# TAKE ME THERE

# TAKE ME THERE
## oasis THE STORY

**PAUL MATHUR**
Introductions by Noel & Liam Gallagher

BLOOMSBURY

First published in Great Britain 1996
This paperback edition first published 1997
Bloomsbury Publishing Plc, 38 Soho Square, London W1V 5DF

A CIP catalogue record for this book
is available from the British Library

ISBN 0 7475 3388 1

10 9 8 7 6 5 4 3 2 1

Typeset by Palimpsest Book Production Limited,
Polmont, Stirlingshire
Printed and bound in Great Britain by
Clays Ltd, St Ives plc

# SPECIAL THANKS

Oasis, Alan McGee, Johnny Hopkins and everyone at Creation; Marcus, Christine and all at Ignition; Penny Phillips and Jocasta Brownlee at Bloomsbury; Brian, Matt, Martin & Andy at microdot; Tom Sheehan, Meg Mathews, Simon Mason, Ben Stud, Patsy Kensit, Lucy Woollard, Stephanie Sammut, Jennifer Dale Crisafulli, Emma from Underworld, Bobby G & Duffy, Richard Dawes, Jennifer Roberts, Robbie Williams, Paul Weller, Johnny Marr, Owen Morris, Richard Ashcroft, John, Keith, Skin & Pete; Jason Rhodes, Roger Nowell, Martin Carr, Tony Judge, Polly Gordon, Dom Stud, Emma Moon, Mum and Dad, Anita, Lisa Moorish, Zoe Shardlow, Tessa Jowers, Peggy Gallagher, Paul Gallagher, Terry O'Neill, Kevin Camp, Mick Flindell, Tim & Chris Abbot, Smaller, Real People and loads of others.

You know.

For R.C.

Live Forever

# CONTENTS

# NOEL GALLAGHER

What's it like being Noel Gallagher in 1996? I don't know. To be honest with you, it's not a lot different from what it was like a year ago. It just seems to keep on getting better.

What's happened with Oasis has given me more than anything else a chance to be able to do what I do without having to worry about not having any money. If ten years ago you had asked me to imagine anything like this it would have been completely beyond my imagination. I'm sure it was the same for all of us. We knew what we wanted, but none of us ever expected it could have been as huge as this. But I think a lot of what we've achieved has come about because we've caught the spirit of what was missing in a lot of other people's lives.

I don't know why we've got so big, except for the obvious thing that we've got better songs than anyone else around. And I suppose we still dress and look and think a lot like our fans. They can see a lot of themselves in us. And we've never played those games where you're supposed to suck up to all the pop stars around you. We say exactly what we feel and don't care if it's going to offend anybody. I mean, someone was telling me the other day that I ought to be careful about what I say about other bands 'cos I'm going to have to meet them on the way down. So what? If I meet them on the way down it'll give me a chance to slag them off again then. If other people are dicks, they're always going to be dicks and I'm not going to start pretending otherwise just to keep everyone happy. A lot of things might have changed for us, but we've never taken any shit off people, right from the off. I'm loyal to my mates and I always will be. And they know that. But I'm not going to waste my life kissing the arses of people who mean nothing to me. I think our fans respect that.

Is there a downside to all the fame? Nothing that I can't put up with. I mean, you get recognized when you're shopping, so you just do it on a Sunday morning instead. The biggest thing I've got to worry about is whether I've got a hangover. It's not exactly like I lie awake at night worrying about how I can't travel on buses or anything. I'm writing better than ever and I've got loads more songs inside my head that I want to record. I'll keep on doing this as long as I still get enjoyment from it and I can't see that stopping for a long time yet. Some other band are bound to come along one day and be bigger than us or write better songs than us, but right now I don't see them anywhere. Sometimes I think, well, if anything is going to follow us, then maybe I'll have to invent it.

Mathur has been right there since the start. He was the very first journalist we ever met and we thought he was sound right from the start. He seemed to understand what our enthusiasm was all about and for three years he's heard loads of our songs before anyone else. After we first met him and it seemed like he was really up for it all, we thought every other journalist was going to be like him. Unfortunately we've since found out they're not. Paul's been around us for three years and we still haven't shaken him off. He's one of the few writers I trust. He understands what we're about.

# LIAM GALLAGHER

What am I supposed to write? Ask me some questions.

*Who's Liam Gallagher?*

Me. The singer in the band. The best-looking one.

*What do you want from your life?*

I want to do something that fucking means something to me. I already have. In the future it might be being in a band and it might be chilling out and it might be going off to live in the middle of nowhere. If it's good, I'm mad for it. I don't plan out what I'll be doing in twenty years' time.

*Do you love Noel?*

Yes.

*What about the stories of arguments and stuff?*

I'm arsed.

*Can you write great songs?*

I think I will one day. Right, this is something I want to say. Oasis was my band and right now Noel writes all the songs because he can and I'm happy to sing them, but it doesn't mean I just sit back and think, well, he's going to write all the songs I sing for the rest of my life. I wrote songs when we first started and, all right, they might not have been great, but I really believe that one day, maybe tomorrow, maybe next month, maybe in fucking ten years' time, I'll write something really great and it'll be a fuck off to all those people who say I should just stand in the middle and be the singer. I get all these people telling me about how I should be living my life and how they know what I'm thinking. They know nish. I know what goes on in my head and I know that I can write something that will surprise a lot of people. When I'm ready I'll do it.

*Do you get scared going on stage in front of loads of people?*

Do I fuck. I'm right up for it. If you're going to get scared you shouldn't be doing it. It's not like we've gone from playing to twenty people to playing to loads. At the big gigs I'm buzzing. Yeah, I'm mad for it.

*Would you die for anyone?*

Me.

*Is it good being engaged?*

What do you think? Of course it is or I wouldn't have fucking done it, would I?

*Do you want to read a book about Oasis?*

I'm not bothered. I don't think about what we've done in the past. I'm only interested in what we're doing now. Everyone's going to come along and say 'they did this and they did that' and most of them will be wrong because they weren't even there. They just write about what they read in the papers and that's all written by dickheads.

*What about me?*

Well, you were there right at the beginning with your glasses on the end of your nose and you haven't stitched us up yet, so I suppose you're all right. I liked that bit you wrote once about how I was like a Tasmanian Devil.

*Who do you trust?*

Hardly anyone. If someone is honest with me and doesn't fuck me around, then fine, they're OK. The fans who've been into us from the start, they're all right. I know who means anything to me and they know too. That's all that matters.

# Maine Road, Manchester
# 27 April 1996

It's one hell of a burning sky. Jagged amber spikes puncture the landscape out past the city's suburbs, cascading towards the horizon. In front of you, 40,000 people are having the best moment of their lives, turning every dream you ever had into some sort of eternally incomprehensible reality. It's all about you, about everything you do, blown up on to hundred-foot screens behind your head. You look out at all the people, wonder for half a second whether they're really all here just to see you.

Of course they are.

You watch the world revolve around you as the dusk eases into a spotlight-studded darkness.

This is it. Forever.

You're Oasis. And you're everything.

# 1

## BURNAGE BOYS

Right time, right place – it matters. And you couldn't get much more of a right time or right place than the North of England in the mid-sixties. Postwar regeneration made the area the focus of a new industrial dream, the cities expanding to accommodate what would turn out to be the country's last, hopeless surge of economic optimism. Manchester and Liverpool were at the heart of the dream, strengthened by the glamour of pop music and football, playgrounds for the newly defined teenage abandon. Worlds where anything was possible. If only.

In fact, by '67 the bands had all moved to London, the life of the superstar footballer was still resiliently elusive to all but a very few, and poverty drenched everyday existence with the same dulling regularity as the pouring rain. The dream might have flickered for a moment, but as the seventies approached, peace and love didn't count for much round Manchester way.

Burnage was typical of the city's newly created suburbs, a place designed to accommodate the overspill from overcrowded districts closer to the centre, like Moss Side and Hulme. Neat rows of houses, the luxury of gardens and the promise of somewhere to live rather than just to exist. Just an illusion, of course. The boredom and the despair and the crime don't go away simply because you paper over a few cracks. Burnage was by no means the worst part of Manchester, but neither was it some sort of problem-free safe haven.

Peggy Gallagher and her husband Thomas were typical of the Irish Catholic population prevalent in Manchester. Decent family values, hard work to make ends meet, and a fierce loyalty to their roots. Well, for Peggy at least. There were three kids: Paul, the eldest by a year, was followed by Noel on 29 May 1967, and William (who didn't like his first name and preferred to be called Liam) on 21 September 1972.

Neither Noel nor Liam was a pillar of the community, Liam's hyperactivity even driving one of his primary-school teachers at St Bernard's, Burnage Lane, to take an aspirin every day after he'd been in one of her lessons. Meanwhile Noel, who was growing up as quickly as such a tough environment demands, was soon wagging school, getting into drugs, specifically glue and dope. He virtually gave up on lessons, not helped by his dyslexia, a learning difficulty which at that time wasn't looked at with much sympathy at any school in the country, let alone in a Catholic establishment where just keeping everyone in line was the basic rationale.

Noel even managed to get in trouble on his last day at school, when an attempt to wreak revenge on the school bully ended in a badly aimed bag of flour covering the headmaster. He was expelled without an official leaving certificate. Not that he cared.

Liam started at the same school, Barlow Roman Catholic High School, in East Didsbury, just after Noel had left, his physi-cal resemblance to Noel ensuring that he got all the stick for his brother's previous misdemeanours. Liam might have been bothered if he had cared any more about his education than Noel had, but he found none of his schooldays the slightest bit inspirational. When he was fifteen, he was, as usual, 'standing around on a corner smoking a fag', when he got caught up in a fight between fellow pupils and those from a nearby rival school. He still maintains his innocence, but shortly afterwards sacked the lessons for ever and got a job making fences.

Peggy was working at the local McVitie's biscuit factory, spending her days sorting out the misshapes.

'That's what you used to get fed,' Noel has said. 'Come home from school and you'd have two ham sandwiches, a tiny little bottle of milk and about sixty Penguins and seventy Jaffa Cakes. Made you dead popular at school, though: "Here comes Gallagher the Biscuit."'

Thomas Gallagher had a job making concrete floors and working part-time as a Country and Western DJ, dragging Noel around pubs from an early age to help set up the equipment. Noel remembers it all as completely boring, stuck in the corner with a bag of crisps and a Coke. The first record Thomas bought Noel was Leo Sayer's 'The Show Must Go On'. If only he'd known how apt the title would be for his son's future career. However, Noel did teach himself to play his father's guitar. Too small to see over it at first, he had to learn with it flat on his lap. Also, he played right-handed, going against his natural left-handedness. When he was thirteen he was allowed his own guitar and ordered a cheap copy of a black Gibson Hummingbird from a catalogue. Having been grounded for six months after a glue-fuelled attempt to rob a corner shop, he had plenty of time to practise, teaching himself three chords and running through endless versions of 'Ticket To Ride' and 'House Of The Rising Sun'.

Around the same time, he lost his virginity (something else that his all-boys school wasn't about to give him any help with). As he and the girl were fumbling about on the bed, there was a knock at the door that they ignored until they'd finished. The knock turned out to have been the last, desperate plea from the local dustman for someone to call an ambulance as he had a heart attack on the front doorstep.

Noel had been inspired by punk, as much for its rebellious stance as the raw power of groups like the Sex Pistols, whose *Never Mind The Bollocks* was the first record he ever bought himself. In 1980, though, he finally got to his first gig: the Damned at Manchester Apollo. He was excited by the atmosphere, but not enough to go and pogo down at the front. He filed the experience away under 'interesting' and went back to playing his guitar in his room. Shortly afterwards, he wrote his first song, 'Badge'. The best line, he would later tell Miranda Sawyer from the *Observer*, went: 'And on your badge it says, "Wear A Badge".' Not perhaps destined for the Greatest Hits album, but an indication of how early Noel recognized the only way he was ever going to do anything with the thoughts inside his head.

He certainly wasn't going to achieve anything working on building sites, as he did with both brothers, his father and a host of cousins, from an early age. Long days spent arguing in the rain would drag on into the inevitable scraps at home – something that only ended when, sick of all the abuse, he fought back and hospitalized his father. He has only seen him once in the ten years since then, as Peggy and her three sons had moved by the time his injuries had healed and he'd been discharged.

'He turned up a year ago saying he wanted to make up for things,' says Noel. 'Then he tried to sell a newspaper a bit of paper with a song I'd written on it when I was fourteen or something. That's so typical of him. We'll never make up with him. I don't even think about him.'

If there was a single act that crystallized Noel's desire to make music, it was the Smiths. He'd seen them on *Top Of The Pops* and been transfixed by Johnny Marr, seeing in the guitarist so much of what he himself wanted to be. After he went to see them at Manchester Free Trade Hall in 1984, he was more convinced than ever. Smiths pictures and records joined those of the Jam and the Beatles in the room that he shared with Liam, a room that soon became a jumble of guitars and recording equipment.

Liam, though, wasn't the slightest bit interested in music.

'I just couldn't see the point,' he explains. 'I didn't get it. If I saw someone with a guitar I'd just laugh at them. It seemed such a stupid thing to want to do, play music. I just went out and had a good time, getting pissed up or whatever, chasing girls.'

Noel continued to build up his record collection, getting most of his stuff from Sifter's in Fog Lane, Didsbury, the shop that would later be immortalized in 'Shakermaker'. The owner, Peter Howard, the man who would become 'Mr Sifter' in the song, recalls Noel coming in and buying everything from 'golden oldies' to stuff by Adam & the Ants (Noel considers their 'Car Trouble' to be one of the songs he always wishes he'd written). Howard would joke about the Beatles' saying they were bigger than Jesus, and warned Noel to be careful about what he said to the press if he ever got famous. Wise advice, as it turned out.

Liam was eventually convinced of the point of rock 'n' roll when he and Noel went to see the Stone Roses in Manchester in 1988.

'It changed my life,' Liam says now. 'I saw Ian Brown on stage and he was singing off-key and everything, but it just got to me. Then when he went off it was like he'd taken a bit of me with him. And after that I was mad for listening to music, getting into it. I knew I wanted to be in a band.'

So did Noel. He'd been working at a variety of dead-end jobs as a labourer, baker, signwriter, even a fish-tank maker, and had ended up working for a building firm subcontracted to British Gas. At work one day he dropped the cap off a huge pipe on to his foot, breaking bones and earning himself sick leave. When he returned he was given a job in a storeroom, a place where he'd be lucky to see a couple of people a week at most. Before long he started taking his guitar in and writing songs to while away the boredom. It was there that he wrote four songs that would appear on the *Definitely Maybe* album, including 'Live Forever', which was written about, and for, his mum.

He describes the injury to his foot as 'a pivotal moment in my life'.

Realizing his burgeoning talents as a songwriter, he decided he wanted to sing in a band. At the Stone Roses gig he had met a guy called Clint Boon, who was bootlegging it, and the two had bumped into each other a few times since then. When Boon revealed that there was a vacancy for a singer in his band, Inspiral Carpets, Noel decided to give it a go. And so, at the end of December 1988, on the night of the Lockerbie air disaster, Noel bowled along to the band's studio, The Mill, in Ashton-under-Lyne, to audition as their new singer.

He played them tapes of his renditions of Inspiral Carpets songs, 'Joe', 'Whiskey' and 'Keep The Circle Around', as well as a cover of the Stones' 'Gimme Shelter', but he didn't have the vibe they were looking for. They did, however, offer him a job as their roadie.

'Our mum has never stopped us doing what we want to do,' says Noel. 'She might not have liked it, but she always supported us.'

And, while the music industry was a completely strange world to her, she was impressed by the fact that her son was getting to travel the world and make good money.

It gave Noel a chance to cock his nose at the headmaster who'd always told him he'd never make anything of his life. When he was booked to travel to America with Inspiral Carpets, he had to go to his old headmaster to get his application form for a visa signed, and he took great pleasure in mentioning that he was earning £600 a week. Quite some way of not making anything of his life.

As well as the USA, Noel got to travel to Argentina, Russia and Japan, an invaluable experience for what was to lie ahead of him.

'That's why I've never been as mad as the others on tour,' says Noel. 'I got all the stuff about going wild and getting off with the girls and everything out of the way early on with the Inspirals. And I was watching everything that was going on, seeing them doing interviews and dealing with the record company people.'

Sometimes he'd even do interviews, pretending to be one of the band, usually when Clint was too hung-over to turn up himself. The rest of the time he bided his time, watched and waited. He also built up a close friendship with Mark Coyle, the Inspirals' monitor engineer and future Oasis producer. Often, during sound checks, the two would play Noel's newly written songs together and, for a few moments at least, Gallagher could imagine what it would be like to be doing it for real.

It was while on tour with Inspiral Carpets that Noel had his one and only experience of sprinkling cocaine on his cornflakes, an episode that would later be wrongly attributed to Oasis. About to fly back to Britain from abroad and finding themselves with an unfeasibly bulging stash, Noel and Coyle decided on a desperate course of action. Covering their breakfast cereal with coke, they managed a mouthful each before comprehending just why it wasn't the most manageable or popular form of narcotic ingestion. They never did it again.

Liam, meanwhile, was looking for his own chance to become a rock 'n' roll star, and opportunity was just about to come to the door armed with a sledgehammer.

The Gallaghers had hung around in the local Errwood Road park with a couple of dozen equally delinquently inclined mates, necking magic mushrooms, stealing milk floats and generally pushing out the envelope of teenage mayhem. Among their compadres were Paul 'Guigs' McGuigan, Tony McCarroll and Paul Arthurs, the latter having been known since childhood as Bonehead. The three of them had formed a band called Rain, along with a singer whose name no one is prepared to reveal. Apparently just as well, since he was the weak link in a chain that was hardly strong anyway.

'Rain were really, really sad,' says Bonehead. 'Absolutely terrible. I had this weird long hair, bald on top, and Guigs was really fat. We did cover versions of songs like "Wild Thing", playing these shit gigs round Manchester, going nowhere. Eventually we sacked the singer, which wasn't exactly a smart move 'cos none of the rest of us could sing. So we were looking for a replacement and someone said, "Have you heard Noel's brother Liam? He sings a bit." So we got him along to an audition and he was really good. We thought, right, let's have him in the band. Maybe we can really do something.'

With the fresh start came a name change. Rain was gone and Oasis was born.

The name's origins have been the subject of a host of explanations, and the band themselves tend to come up with a different story for every interview. They've said in the past that it came from the name of a Manchester shop that sold trainers to the local hooligans; that it was the name of a Burnage cab firm; that it was a curry house just around the corner from Bonehead's; even that it had some obscure connection with the Beatles. In fact, it came about when Noel roadied for Inspiral Carpets at a venue in Swindon called Oasis. Liam liked the name and the resonance of its imagery. So, even though people kept on telling them it sounded as if they were a reggae band, Oasis it was.

The freshly christened band spent each weekend in the basement of the Boardwalk, a small local venue in Little Peter Street near the Hacienda club. The subterranean rehearsal rooms under the venue were used by many of the city's fledgeling acts, and Oasis were soon regulars, hammering away with more enthusiasm than promise of excellence. Nevertheless, on 18 August 1991, they were finally ready for their first gig, upstairs at the Boardwalk itself, supporting a group called Sweet Jesus.

Noel was in the audience, tipped off by his mother that Liam was in a band. When he saw them that night, he thought they were 'completely shit', but also realized that his brother's stage presence showed great promise. The band asked Noel if he'd be their manager, but he had something bigger and better in mind.

'I went up to them,' he says, 'and I told them, "I don't want to be your manager, but how about I join the band? If I do, then we do things my way, play my songs, rehearse every night. And I guarantee we'll be the biggest band in the world." I knew by then that all I wanted to do was have a band, make a record, get my name in brackets. When I played them "Live Forever", they knew I was right.'

And so, now a five-piece, Oasis prepared for world domination. Something that didn't prove quite as easy as Noel had imagined.

The new-look Oasis played their first gig on 19 October 1991, again at the Boardwalk. They played four songs: a cover of a house song inspired by Noel's love of the Acid House scene, and three original compositions, 'Take Me' (written by Liam and Bonehead), 'Columbia' and an acoustic song called, funnily enough, 'Acoustic Song'. There were only twenty people there, and most of their mates who'd come along had refused to pay on the door, but it was a start.

The band had put together a couple of roughly recorded demo tapes and set about getting a record deal. One of the first people they approached was Tony Wilson, head of Manchester-based Factory Records. While he was approachable and enthusiastic at the band's first meeting with him, he rang them a couple of weeks later to say that their tape was too heavily influenced by the 'baggy' scene that had led to Manchester being rechristened 'Madchester'. He wasn't interested in signing them.

Unperturbed, Noel continued to send out tapes, giving one to

Macca, manager of local band Northside. Macca, who works these days with the Lightning Seeds, was impressed enough to recommend them to the producers of the *Hit The North* radio show, earning the band a session on the programme. It could have been the real start of something, particularly as the band played the newly initiated 'In The City' music industry event a week later. They were genuinely shocked when they were ignored by all record company A&R men. It had been almost a year since the first gig with Noel in the band, and they were no nearer to their dream.

But they were still convinced of their own ability, and Noel upped the frequency of their rehearsals and set about organizing a proper demo tape. The latter came thanks to the benevolence of Liverpool band the Real People, whom Noel had first seen supporting Inspiral Carpets. Sharing Oasis's desire to make classic pop, they offered free use of their studio in Liverpool's Dock Road, and helped them out with the practicalities of working in a studio. The resulting demo was the best thing Oasis had done to date and the first to capture the ferocity of their intent.

Noel had a mate called Ian, who was an actor. During one late-night conversation, Ian said he'd give an Oasis tape to his brother, who might be interested.

'I was, like, "Why the fuck would your brother be interested in our tape?" says Noel. 'And he goes, "Oh, my brother's Johnny Marr." I never knew. I went, yeah, give him the tape, definitely. Go and do it now. I didn't expect anything to come of it, but I wanted him to hear it.'

Johnny Marr loved the tape and rang up suggesting a meeting. Noel was gobsmacked by his reaction.

'He went, "Let's meet up", and I was trying to be calm, saying, "Hey, why not", but I was shitting myself. Anyway I met up with him and we got on really well. We were talking about guitars and I told him about how I had this brown 1970 Epiphone Riviera, a real classic that I'd bought at this shop in Doncaster. He was as mad as me on guitars and thought he knew every shop in the country, but he hadn't heard of this one, so he goes, "Let's drive there now." So we did.'

The two walked into the Doncaster shop, called Music Ground, and Marr immediately spent £9000 on guitars.

'When he did that,' says Noel, 'I thought, that should be me doing that. That's what I want.'

Marr's support alerted his own manager, Marcus Russell, to the band, and Oasis themselves started to exhibit a fresh self-belief. Their gigs were still sparsely attended, but the group had begun to visualize the possibilities and they weren't about to countenance the prospect of failure. At one gig, no one at all turned up, but Oasis went ahead with their set, even going so far as to do an encore.

'We were brilliant,' says Noel. 'It didn't matter that no one was there.'

By early 1993 it was obvious, at least to the band, that they really could be successful. Noel stopped smoking dope and wrote fifty songs in two weeks. All they needed now was a break.

# 2

## CREATION AND FAITH

Oasis wanted the world. The band's current success might suggest that they'd have got it wherever they went, however they'd chosen to storm the barricades of success. Hindsight, with its eternally overrated twenty-twenty vision, points out that tiny signpost marked 'OASIS – A PHENOMENON JUST WAITING TO HAPPEN'. And every pony-tailed executive in every office in every company all over the world lies awake at night, bites the pillow and says, 'Yeah, I could have done that. I could have made them what they are. Oasis sold themselves. Easy.'

He never gets to sleep till dawn. No way.

Actually, there is a microscopic element of truth in the suggestion that Oasis would have been huge if they'd signed to a different label; that everything they've done is entirely of their own making, totally self-sufficient. And, as the first person to champion them in the music press, I've never pretended, even to myself, that any contribution I've made has done anything more than hasten their rise by a couple of months.

In an early piece about them in *Melody Maker* I wrote, 'I don't care if they're the best fucking band in your world, they're the

13

best in mine.' As they roar gorgeously beyond even my hyperbolic expectations, it's a mantra that still holds true, an often paper-thin assertion that keeps the madness just far enough away. Loving them is never an afterthought.

Most importantly, that holds for everybody who works with them. They're supported with a genuine passion by the people in charge of the selling of the surge. And that's what the pony-tailed pimps will never understand. It's not about units or market shares or treating diamonds like another brand of dog food. It's about a genuine, unashamed love. About surfing heartbeats.

Alan McGee understood. Right from the start. He had been understanding the rock 'n' roll impulse for a decade: personal inspirations communicated with a bold, reckless energy through his own label, Creation Records. Oasis were to be his most important discovery, the band that would set him up financially for life, but their very existence owed a lot to the musical environment that he himself had exuberantly nurtured.

A defiant disregard for conventional business sense and some-thing of an overemphasis on the 'recreational' side of sending out a message to the world, had ensured that Creation spent much of its first ten years lurching between ragged glory and an appointment with the Official Receiver. Some sort of security was established only in 1992, via a lucrative deal with Sony. Creation would have probably still been around if Oasis had never existed. If, however, Creation hadn't kept on hurtling through ten years of unshakeable self-belief, Oasis, no matter what they might have thought, probably wouldn't have even dreamed about being around in the first place.

'I wasn't one of those big Creation fans who went out and bought all the records they put out,' maintains Noel. 'I mean, they had some really, really shit acts. People like Shonen Knife. I was aware of Primal Scream and all that lot, though, and I have to admit that Alan McGee always makes you think he completely believes in anyone he's signed. He obviously had a track record.'

Back in the early eighties, the only tracks that McGee was supposed to think about were the ones with trains on them. Having moved from his native Glasgow to London, he was working by day for British Rail, playing at night in a group call the Laughing Apple (also featuring Andrew Innes, who was to go on to play guitar in Primal Scream). He was also using his £72 weekly wages to promote a couple of clubs called Communication! and the Living Room, putting on gigs by most of his mates.

'I've never gone out to just make a lot of money,' says McGee. 'When I was working for British Rail I knew what I was earning and I reckoned if I could earn the same or a bit more doing something I enjoyed then it had to be worth it.'

In August 1983 Alan McGee put a single out by the Legend, known since by another of his pseudonyms, Everett True, currently the Assistant Editor of *Melody Maker*. The Legend's ''73 In '83' didn't exactly send philosophers or rock historians scurrying for their correction fluid, but it was a suitably impulsive starting-point for McGee's assault on the way you were supposed to go about being a magnate. ''73 In '83' remains a sporadically sought-after item, its rarity compounded by the fact that McGee kept most of the unsold copies under his bed, and when, a few years later, he fell out with the Legend, he burnt them all. Just for the sake of it.

'We only sold forty-seven copies of that single,' says McGee, 'but I thought, well, let's do another.'

And so began a regularly haphazard contribution to post-punk musical culture. The first few releases seemed only to reiterate a whimsical loyalty to his best mates and while the likes of Revolving Paint Dream, Biff Bang Pow! (McGee himself in a none-too-successful disguise) and Jasmine Minks and the Pastels have all since garnered a dreamily obsessive acclaim of sorts, Creation wasn't about to walk away with any awards for innovation.

All that changed with the Jesus and Mary Chain. McGee had heard their demos on the B-side of one of his friend Bobby

Gillespie's bootleg Syd Barrett tapes and went along to check them out in the studio. At first he thought that they sounded like some sort of limp, home-grown version of the Ramones, but when they turned the feedback up so high that the melodies were all but obliterated, he sensed a marvellously uncompromising potential. The Jesus and Mary Chain embarked on a series of gorgeously cacophonous performances, never playing for more than twenty minutes and ensuring that both critics and punters redefined any idea of expectation. The band's first single for Creation, 'Upside Down', sold 50,000 in three months and reintroduced a celebration of the brazenly uncomfortable to the musical arena. While inevitably operating on the periphery, Creation and the Jesus and Mary Chain couldn't hope to make any sort of impact on the mainstream, but, for anyone who was interested in exploring pop's edges, they roared out a whole new pack of possibilities.

In 1985 the Jesus and Mary Chain signed to Blanco Y Negro, a label initially allied with fellow independent Rough Trade and later picked up by the multinational WEA. McGee managed them and admits that he found himself caught up in the excitement of a hands-on involvement with the band that the music press were pinpointing as Rock's Last Gasp.

'It was brilliant,' says McGee. 'There'd be riots at gigs, complete chaos. We were winding everyone up with all these claims that the band were Art Terrorists and then, whenever they played, it'd be mayhem. We were just taking the piss, but it got really scary. And exciting at the same time.'

While the walls came tumbling down, creation carried on putting out records by the increasingly wussy-sounding Pastels and, as a nod to the aspirations of pal Bobby Gillespie, a couple of singles by his band Primal Scream.

Gillespie was one of McGee's oldest friends. Indeed, in 1975, it was to McGee that he had turned, knocking on his door and asking him to take him along to his first rock concert, a Thin Lizzy gig. In the early days of the Living Room, McGee put on Primal Scream's first gig.

The release by Creation of Primal Scream's singles, 'All Fall Down' and 'Velocity Girl', established them as cornerstones for the self-styled 'C86' movement, a genre marked out by the incessant jangle of self-consciously throwaway melodies and self-regarding innocence as a viable, allegedly invigorating option.

While ostensibly sanctifying the pursuit of melody, at the same time Creation continued to release records by the likes of Meat Whiplash and Slaughter Joe. Terrifically nasty reworkings of noise as an enduring aesthetic.

'I just put out songs I liked,' says McGee. 'That's what I've always done and what I'm going to keep on doing. Once you start to put out stuff 'cos you think it's fashionable or what you're supposed to do, you might as well just forget why you're doing it in the first place.

'For the first couple of years, I was doing the label because I wanted to put out things I liked. Nothing more. Then it got to the stage where it had definitely become a business, not just a hobby.'

Problems first arose when he tried to trade his facility for talent-spotting against an admirably stubborn faith in artists that he knew were never going to top charts but who he thought deserved to make records. And so in 1987 he set up a label called Elevation, operating through WEA and, in his mind, existing mainly to fund a Creation LP by a group called the Weather Prophets. Leaping into bed with a major was to introduce him to a whole new world of corporate wheeler-dealing, a world where his single-minded idealism was torn apart, forced into debilitating compromise. Within months his marriage had broken up and he found himself 'broke and disillusioned'.

'Elevation was a disaster,' he has since admitted to *Select* magazine. 'It taught me that I have to have total control over what happens to my groups. I moved to Brighton about the same time as the Primals because Bobby said the seaside'd be good for us. That's when I really started being serious about the label as a business. I turned twenty-eight years old and suddenly I thought I'd better do something with my life.'

Nineteen eighty-eight saw Creation starting afresh, or at least capitalizing on McGee's ability to encourage innovative impulses that set their own agenda rather than limping around predefined borders. A compilation called 'Doing It For The Kids' didn't transcend its title – it merely reiterated the label's original intent, giving an audience the guitar-led vivaciousness of House Of Love, the prodigious horizon busting of My Bloody Valentine and the reliably focused peculiarity of Felt. Musically, the label resisted anything even approaching an in-house sound, but it confidently supported a commitment to the extraordinary. When Phonogram leapt in to sign House Of Love for £400,000, McGee stoically resigned himself to the fact that they'd smother a genuine songwriting talent, confident that Creation still had a roster that was capable of mixing it with the big boys. Underrated dance-inspired projects released under the banners of Hypnotone and the Love Corporation hinted at a bold determination to embrace the dizzying power of Acid House.

'You'd go into the Hacienda in Manchester back then,' says Alan, 'and it was just like punk all over again. There'd be all these people completely off their heads on E and this incredible energy about the whole thing. I'm sure the drugs had a lot to do with it, but I just threw myself into the whole Acid House scene for the next three months. I wanted the bands on the label to start making everything a lot weirder, just going for it.'

The most significant moment and one that would define much of the basis for the sound of the next decade came when DJ Andy Weatherall was let loose on remixing a Primal Scream track intended as a B-side to their 'I'm Losing More Than I'll Ever Have'. Weatherall was a fan and a friend of the band who'd written a review of one of their gigs for the *NME*. He'd never remixed anything before, but had a lot of ideas and sensed the sparkle of a completely new direction. The result was 'Loaded'.

'Loaded' remains one of the most important rock records ever released. Born out of a conventional guitar song, it was shaped by Weatherall into a hypnotic, overwhelmingly modern dance groove, almost all the vocals removed save for a Peter Fonda sample extolling the single-minded pursuit of hedonistic oblivion. Inspired by the open-minded 'Balearic' sound that Andy Weatherall would play at Boys Own parties and clubs like Shoom, Rip and Land Of Oz, it created a completely original rock/dance interface as well as a feeling that anything was possible.

It was Creation's first Top Ten hit.

The ensuing Primal Scream album, *Screamadelica*, merely consolidated the band's status as sonic visionaries, taking the energy and excitement of a 'proper' band playing rock and deflecting it through dance, dub and soulful balladeering. It sold half a million worldwide and topped most of the critical end-of-year charts.

Meanwhile Creation had built themselves a startling roster. Teenage Fan Club and Ride ('I nicked them from another label as soon as I heard a tape in the A&R man's office') both made assured, inventive albums, soon followed by Sugar and the Boo Radleys.

Despite the commercial and critical success, the label continued to operate on a shoestring.

'It was no one's fault, but our own,' admits McGee. 'We just didn't have any kind of business sense. The My Bloody Valentine album cost a lot and all the dealings with them were driving me to a nervous breakdown, but I can't blame them for the financial problems we were having. It was all down to the way that we were treating it all just like when we first started. It was like we were trading out of a cardboard box.'

Creation were bleeding badly, despite having three of the world's most successful albums – certainly, along with Nirvana's debut, the most subculturally influential. A quick solution was required and in 1991 they made what was to prove to be one major error of judgement by signing a deal with SBK Records. In return for half a million pounds, Creation gave SBK first option in America on all Creation acts not already licensed in the US.

'It was just a practical solution,' maintains McGee. 'We had to face the fact that we needed money quick and the SBK deal meant we got it. If we'd waited any longer we'd have gone out of business – as simple as that. Looking back, it obviously caused a lot of problems, but in the short term it stopped us going under.'

Ramifications from that deal continued to hold Creation back for the next few years, even after they'd shifted the debt to Sony in 1992.

'What happened with Sony was that we sold them forty-nine percent of the company and they gave us three and a half million pounds. Me and Dick Green [McGee's business partner in Creation] got to keep fifty-one percent, so we kept a controlling interest, and Sony got worldwide sales for all the great bands. It worked out well for everyone involved because it gave Sony a kind of hip credibility they never had before. They could see that Creation was putting out cool stuff and they could establish an association with it.'

The Sony deal took the pressure off Creation and gave them a solid financial base to develop the label, but as they prepared to celebrate their tenth anniversary (deliberately taking the starting point as 1984 and disregarding the 1983 single by the Legend), McGee showed little sign of giving up his party animal crown.

'I look back on it now and I'm surprised at just how crazy it had all got. I mean I used to just go off to America like I was going down to the pub or something. I remember feeling a bit depressed one day, so I went off to New York for the weekend. I was seeing this model over there and we went out to a gig and took a whole load of acid. By next morning I was still tripping off my box and I knew I had to get something to eat, so I went into this Blimpie and I was, like, the only white person until I looked up and, sitting a few yards away, there was Steven Berkoff. I thought I was still tripping, but it turned out it was really him. I went through a lot of very odd years.'

In early 1994 McGee was still partying hard and maintaining his label's reputation for an almost ludicrous sense of spectacle. Agreeing to an interview with Keith Cameron of the *NME* that reviewed Creation's first decade, he decided against London, but invited him to LA's Mondrian Hotel, where he reminisced through a haze of drugs and alcohol. Despite the narcotically fuelled self-confidence, he managed some perceptive self-analysis. 'For the first six years I was a total chancer,' he said. 'I blagged it. All I did was keep choosing the right band and try not to fuck it up too much, which I usually did. I think about four years ago I started adding to the whole thing rather than detracting, but nobody taught me to run a record company and I've made millions of mistakes.'

McGee was full of optimism and Cameron got it spot on when he described him as 'like your idiot cousin who insists on jumping off bridges for a laugh, but will occasionally bring home a gold nugget from the river mud'.

The day-to-day running of Creation was as eccentric as ever and McGee admits that 'each day we'd wait until five-thirty, then go downstairs, chop out a load of lines and head off to the pub, then stay out until four in the morning. Every night.' Perhaps some of his exuberance came from the fact that he was sitting on a deal with the band that were to change a million lives. He'd got Oasis and his future was about to explode into gold dust.

'I actually met Noel for the first time in 1989,' he recalls. 'I was at the Reading Festival and I knew this girl called Louise. We bumped into each other and she introduced me to her boyfriend, so I said hello. It was only later that I realized that the boyfriend was Noel. We just shook hands, talked for a bit, then went off and did whatever we were doing. It wasn't like there were electric sparks when we shook hands or anything. It was only afterwards that I realized it must have been Noel I met.

'Then I went up to Manchester in September 1992 to see this girl I knew in a band called Sister Lovers. She's called Debbie Turner. We were at the Boardwalk and went downstairs to the rehearsal rooms 'cos everyone was chopping out or rolling spliffs or whatever. We went into this room where they rehearsed and there was this huge Union Jack on one wall.'

It was the backdrop to their logo, a nod in the direction of their love of sixties iconography.

'Then, on 31 May 1993, I was in Glasgow,' continues McGee. 'I'd gone to see my sister and a band of mine on Creation, 18 Wheeler, were playing with Sister Lovers at this place called King Tut's Wah Wah Hut. I'd been promising Debbie I'd go along and see her band, so it seemed like a good time to go along. The only thing was, it was a bank holiday weekend, a Sunday, I think, and I had this idea that everything was going to start and finish really early. I turned up at eight-thirty and the guy at the door told me nothing was going to happen until ten.'

Or so the posters said.

Oasis had decided to play a gig in Glasgow. Hitching (or demanding) a lift with Sister Lovers, they turned up at the venue and told the promoter they were going to go on at the bottom of the bill.

'Like fuck you are,' the promoter said. So, for perhaps the only time in their existence, they calculatedly played the Manc scally card.

'We're going to play or we'll trash the place,' said Bonehead.

'Yeah,' said Noel.

Liam did 'the Look'.

'OK,' said the promoter, uniquely unused to threats of violence in Glasgow. 'But make it quick. Four songs, that's all.'

'I'd got there really early,' says McGee, 'but I thought I might as well go in for a drink. As soon as I walked in I saw these kids sitting around a table and they all looked brilliant, dressed in cagoules and stuff. One of them was dressed in white and looked brilliant, like a natural star. They were just sitting around, laughing, having a good time. A bit later, before anyone was supposed to play, this band came on. I didn't know what they were called or anything about them.'

'We genuinely didn't know Alan McGee was going to be there,' says Noel. 'I'd vaguely heard of him and I knew about Creation, but the only reason we went there was 'cos we were bored. We wanted to play to some Scottish cunts.'

'They came on,' says McGee, 'and I realized it was the people I'd seen sitting at the table. The guy in white was the singer and he looked even better onstage than he did sitting down. He looked like he was born to be onstage. They did four songs. "Cloudburst" was first and it was brilliant. There was only me, my sister and a couple of 18 Wheeler there and they were playing like the place was packed. The last song they did was the cover of "I Am The Walrus" and right then I knew I wanted them on Creation.

'They wandered out afterwards,' he remembers, 'and I went up to Noel. I said, "Have you got a record contract?" and he said he hadn't, so I went, "Can I sign you?" I just knew I had to have them on Creation. They were awesome, even then.'

'Like I say, I only knew Creation by name, from people like Primal Scream,' says Noel, 'but this guy was, like, frothing at the mouth. He was so excited. And he was the first person who actually seemed to realize how good we were.'

'18 Wheeler didn't seem to think much of them,' says McGee. 'They were going, "Why do you want to sign those scallies? Sister Lovers are much better." That's mad Glaswegians for you.'

Johnny Hopkins, the man who was to be their press officer, remembers how he first heard about Oasis.

'It must have been an hour or two after the gig,' he remembers. 'I was lying in bed at home in London and the phone rang. It was Alan calling from Glasgow and he just kind of burbled about this band he'd just seen and how they were going to be the greatest band in the world.

'Alan is incredibly enthusiastic about music and middle-of-the-night calls from him about some great band or another were so common that I took the initial call with a pinch of salt. Anyway I'd lost faith in rock 'n' roll and lost my head to house and techno. To me, Primal Scream were the last great rock 'n' roll band and I was sure there would never be a group as good as them again. So I just said, "Alan, call me back in the morning." It turns out he made calls to Tim, Dick, Martin Carr and others that night – he must have had some phone bill.

'An hour later he rang back again and kept carrying on about this band. He must have rung about four or five times that night. Eventually I said, "OK Alan, let me hear something."'

Two days later an Oasis tape arrived at Creation.

'I had loads of meetings that day, so I only heard "Bring It On Down". It was a great statement of intent and sounded like the Stooges and the Pistols, but didn't show the band's diversity. When I took the tape home that night and heard "Columbia", "Married With Children" and "Rock 'n' Roll Star", I was completely sold, frothing at the mouth – the lot. The next day they turned up at work, and the last piece of the jigsaw fell into place.'

The old Creation offices were hunched above a clothing sweat-shop in Hackney, crammed up against pubs full of strippers offering 'Happy Hours' and cafés full of poorly paid Taiwanese expatriates with pinpricked fingers. Sequins and thread set the agenda and the grubby badge of desperation always accompanied you as a souvenir if you so much as passed on a bus. The sort of place that knee-jerk genericists would pinpoint as prime Oasis territory.

'Bonehead came down in his BMW with Noel and Liam,' says Hopkins. 'For starters I was dead impressed that Bonehead had a BMW. Typical Mancs, I thought. They came up to the press office and sort of huddled in the middle of the room. They looked brilliant and they were just sort of bouncing comments off each other, loads of wisecracks, like that old footage you see of Beatles press conferences. They looked like stars right back then. They were a bit edgy – nerves or something – but they had total belief in their abilities. There was a buzz in the building from the moment they walked in.'

'They came up to the offices,' recalls McGee, 'and I had all these pictures on the wall of Gram Parsons, people like that – all my heroes. Noel was looking at them all and when we started talking he was saying how much he liked them, how he had all their records. I was rushing around going to people, "This is brilliant, he understands what we're on about, what great music is. He's my soul brother!" Later on I found out he'd been bullshitting and he'd never heard of half of the people in his life. I have to tell you I was really sad when I found that out. I'd thought, yeah, me, Bobby Gillespie and Noel Gallagher, we know about who was really great. It's just as well he had so many good songs. And I think he really does like most of those people now.'

'Of course I do,' says Noel. 'We had to give it loads of front then, though. You've got to remember we were going in there with this guy who I'd heard of but definitely didn't know really well, and he was offering us a contract. And he seemed sound. He wasn't one of these poncey wankers who just wanted to make a bit of money dead quickly. He was raving about us and even I was, like, "Eh, steady on." He knew how good we could be.'

Oasis were still without a manager and initially they were going to use a guy called Antony Boggiano.

'It didn't seem much of a good idea,' says McGee. 'He didn't seem like he'd be right for it. Then Noel told me about someone called Marcus Russell who was managing Johnny Marr. He'd seen them and liked them and because he'd had a lot of experience they would have someone really solid behind them.

'I didn't know what he'd think of us,' he admits, 'I mean coming into Creation wasn't like coming into any normal record company.

I thought he might think we were a bit kind of mad, which I suppose we were. I think he realized that we had complete belief in Oasis, though, and he started managing them.'

Russell and his management company Ignition were an astute choice. His experience with not only Johnny Marr but also Electronic and The The was to prove invaluable. And the fact that he'd promoted the Sex Pistols' last-ever British gig in the seventies gave a neat sense of continuity to Oasis's place in the musical scheme of things.

A week later Hopkins went to see them play live. McGee had already told him he could be their press officer: 'I thought, Johnny deserves a chance with these. I know he's going to do a good job.'

'They played a gig at a place called the Hop and Grape opposite the University,' says Hopkins. 'Oasis were only the support band, but they came on stage and they just looked fantastic and the songs were great, even better than on the tape. The energy was incredible. They'd brought a few fans with them and they really stuck out among the student audience. There were a few people down the front, but most of the crowd were standing back, hanging around the side of the stage. The one thing I did notice was that almost every girl there was standing staring at Liam with their jaw on the floor. They just couldn't stop staring at him. He was moving about a bit more than he does now and Noel was hanging back a lot more. They commanded the stage. I was blown away. I'd never seen anything like it.'

Over the next few months Hopkins travelled up to Manchester time and time again, watching them play what appeared to be a regular residency at the Hop and Grape.

'The crowds never got any bigger for them,' he says. 'It wasn't like there was any kind of scene in Manchester at the time. The Mondays had gone, the Stone Roses were in Wales and everyone was just listening to dance music. I'd see people walking off to the bar when Oasis were playing and I couldn't understand how they could just walk away. I'd go to their gigs then we'd go clubbing, usually Justin

Robertson's room at Paradise Factory. We'd talk about music and football and there was usually some mayhem. It turned out Noel had been into Acid House, and you can see a similar uplifting positivity in many Oasis tracks. The club connection was crucial from the off. I felt that there were thousands of other disaffected rock fans, who had got into the dance thing but would almost completely get Oasis. Most of the early fans among the writers came from this category. In London we'd all end up at Sabresonic, then on to McGee's flat in Rotherhithe. At these late-night sessions Noel would grab Alan's acoustic and blitz us with new songs. Noel's always been prolific. He'd phone every day to say he'd written a few more songs. He'd play some down the phone and every one was a winner. It'd be, like, "How do you do that, you bastard?" Thing is that, unlike most writers, he's still writing stuff every day and we're nearly three albums down the line. When you hear "The Masterplan" and the rest of the next album you know he's bettering his best.'

Although Creation hadn't yet signed the band, Hopkins decided to play tapes to a few people he thought might be responsive. I was top of the list. And, when the massed ranks of the Creation home guard had finished prising me off the ceiling, it was decided that no one else would hear it for, oh, months.

'I felt it was crucial with a band this special,' says Hopkins, 'to find a writer prepared to leave his safe London cocoon and take a chance on a band he'd never heard. First port of call – the keepers of the faith.'

I'd been writing about pop for years. Growing up in Liverpool, I had started a fanzine that broadcast the delights of the early eighties Liverpool 'scene', consolidation coming through extensive tour-ing/experiencing/ligging with the likes of Teardrop Explodes, Echo & the Bunnymen and Wah! Heat. I'd later embraced the New Pop of ABC, Associates and Funkapolitan, moved through the delights of New Order and the Smiths, the stand-off between Factory and

ZTT for the title of greatest label in the country, the rejuvenating force of the Happy Mondays, Flowered Up and the Stone Roses, the exhilarating swerve that took me towards Acid House and the London underground scene, long, long nights sheltering in the spongy clatter of beautifully dumb beats – all that had convinced me that it was time to stop. I thought I'd worked my way through the menu. Convinced myself that it was time to mosey on out.

I gave myself two weeks before I was going to officially quit.

Then, three days in, Hopkins played me a rough demo of Oasis's 'Cloudburst'.

Thank Christ I had my fingers crossed.

On 14 July 1993 I went up to Manchester to quash the rumours about the demo tape. There may well have only ever been ten copies made. I could well have thought I'd heard eight of the greatest songs ever written. And Oasis might have just been about to bang their heads on the three little piggies flying over Manchester city centre. I wanted proof. Stigmata or nothing.

In the basement under the Boardwalk, a tiny, mossy room with puddles, Oasis took forty minutes to change my life.

They looked ordinary, but in a kind of this-is-the-best-ordinary-ever kind of way. Shyish, friendlyish, happy.

'You can sit there,' said Liam. And they plugged in.

Eight songs later I knew there could never be anything better. Bits of all the great rock I'd heard over the past twenty years reshaped, compacted and flecked with an extraordinary newness, a dazzlingly bright tomorrow. It was like everything and nothing I'd ever heard before. I just knew things would never be the same again. I remember vaguely wondering whether I should clap between songs. And whether the cover of 'I Am The Walrus' had been quite as electric as I'd imagined. And just how something as amazing could have existed without any of us hearing about it.

'We knew you'd got it,' says Noel. 'And you believed everything. I was giving you all this bullshit about how we were going to be the biggest band in the world, better than anyone else ever. And you believed it.'

Yeah, but I was right.

'There is that. You were lucky.'

I was there.

'All right, you can have that. Did you really think we were that good?'

Is the Pope really that Catholic?

'I knew how huge Oasis could and would be,' says Hopkins, 'but I wanted the whole thing to build naturally from a solid base. Too much hype early on kills a band. This band were going to be around for a long time. At that moment I think the way that people were writing about music was more blinkered and less inspiring than it'd been for years. It would have been easy to tell everyone about Oasis straight away, but we could wait. Quite honestly, most people doing the writing wouldn't have got it anyway. The reviews of *Morning Glory* proved that.'

And so, while most other record companies would have dumbly scatter-gunned their latest discovery over every page they could muster, Creation – despite major expenses from the seemingly endless recording sessions for Primal Scream's *Give Out But Don't Give Up* album – decided to keep their latest discovery under wraps until everything was signed. And I'll admit that having gaffer tape over my mouth and being forced to take all food through a straw was character-building. One day, I'll sue.

By now word was spreading fast and almost every record label in the country (including U2's Mother imprint) started slapping offers Oasis's way, many of them promising ludicrously inflated advances. The band resisted, having sensed a spiritual affinity with Creation and being prepared to reward the label for having faith in their assertion that they would be the biggest band in the world. Meanwhile Creation were in negotiation with Sony for worldwide distribution, and while in New York McGee bumped into the one-time Happy Mondays manager Nathan

McGough, at that time earning his money from A&R for WEA.

'Me, Alan and his dad and Dick Green, a Creation director, went out on the piss in New York,' McGough recalled in *VOX* magazine. 'Alan said to me, "I've found the greatest rock 'n' roll band since the Beatles!" I said, "You say that about every fucking band you sign!" And he goes, "No, this time, I mean it."'

A few months later McGough saw Noel sitting outside the Mandela Hall in Manchester and congratulated him on the Creation deal. When Noel revealed that they hadn't actually signed anything yet, he was gobsmacked.

'Being honourable, I just left it at that,' he says. "What I should have said was, "Whatever he's offered, I'll double it."'

McGough wasn't the only person with that thought. Especially after Oasis played a gig on 14 September at Manchester's Canal Bar as part of the In The City Festival. While they didn't win the Best New Band award (that went to the less than luminous Blessed Ethel) they did pick up their first major music press review. The quietly agreed press embargo had been broken via a short mention in the *NME* a couple of weeks earlier and I decided I couldn't hold back any longer. So, on 25 September, in a review of the gig under the heading 'Desert Brats', I let slip that it was 'a night that's quite possibly going to change lives'. This despite the fact that the gig itself was sparsely attended, even if, as with the Pistols at the 100 Club, half the population of Britain now insist they were there. Most of the A&R pack were round the corner at the time watching Shaun Ryder guest at a gig at the University by Intastella. And, while the latter may have been a vaguely perky sideshow, the might of Oasis was clear even then to the hundred or so people who witnessed it.

Dave Massey, who was head of A&R for Sony America, was already convinced. Having heard some demos a couple of months earlier, he'd been blown away. 'I went bonkers,' he says. 'I've never responded to anything before as strongly as I responded to that.' The deal was on. Big time.

# 3

## FIGHTING TALK

If you'd walked into London's Soho Square in late 1993 you'd have found Sony's UK headquarters standing in one corner, suitably looking a bit like a multinational bank. Diagonally opposite you might have spotted Paul McCartney's office. Oasis couldn't have found a more suitable place to sign their record deal even if they'd actually got round to joining the dots in their dreams.

While Oasis had continued to gig during the late summer of 1993, Creation and Marcus Russell had been negotiating behind the scenes with Sony, convinced eventually that the Japanese-owned label would be the best outlet for the irresistible rise of the biggest band in the world. The band themselves were less concerned with corporate negotiation than with the opportunity to finally put out some records.

'We just wanted to start recording some songs,' recalls Bonehead. 'It had all started moving really quickly for us and everyone was going on about record deals, but we were all still dead skint and we wanted to get on with actually recording something. Noel had written loads of songs and we had everything for an album. About ten albums.'

The frustration finally came to an end on the afternoon of 22

October, when Oasis, representatives from Creation and Sony and a few friends all piled into an office at the top of the Sony building to sign the deal that would turn the rock 'n' roll dreams into some sort of explosive reality.

But not before a last-minute alteration to the bit above the dotted line.

On the wall of the office where the contract was to be signed there was a picture of Liverpool band the Farm, the archetypal scally act whose album a year earlier had sold faster than anything since U2's *Rattle And Hum*. While their sound and sensibility had in many ways paved the way for a band like Oasis, Noel decided they were 'a load of shite' and flatly refused to sign any contract until an addendum was added promising that the photo would be turned to face the wall.

'When we signed,' he says, 'I was going to make fucking sure that everything was perfect, and I wasn't going to have those twats looking down on us. I mean, there was Bob Dylan on one wall and us standing there in the middle. The Farm weren't exactly in the same league, if you know what I mean. You've got to have standards, man.'

After the contract was eventually signed, the band resumed their champagne, a crusade that had started at noon. Sony staff unaware of what was going on upstairs found out pretty soon afterwards as toilets, lifts and corridors were overrun by the sort of people who looked, to the drones at least, like they were just about to trash the place. The remains of white lines covered plenty of available surfaces and the dregs from overturned champagne bottles puddled the carpets. Dusk was hours away.

Noel Gallagher leant against a wall, bottle in one hand, cigarette in the other, buzzing off his head, but still a relatively convincing representative of calm at the centre of the maelstrom.

'So, you're rock 'n' roll stars,' I said to him as the room turned into a typhoon-raddled revolving restaurant.

'We've always been rock 'n' roll stars,' he grinned. 'This is fucking brilliant but you haven't seen anything yet. We're going to start proving it.'

Liam ambled by, arms aloft, bottles cascading in his wake, stepping over the Oasis-brand toilet rolls and tinned Jamaican Oasis spinach that I'd brought as a haphazard tribute to the proceedings.

'Let's go out,' he said. 'We're celebrating, right? Let's have it.'

Alan McGee may well, back then, have had little regard for the still, small voice of sobriety, but even he recognized that it was perhaps time to take the rabble-rousing elsewhere. So, waving credit cards at all and sundry, he led everyone down to a Tex-Mex restaurant called Break for the Border, inviting en route a couple of foreign tourists who'd randomly buttonholed us outside Sony and asked if anyone knew where there was a 'condom shop'. Since it was basically devolving into a make-merry free-for-all, a 'fun' restaurant seemed just about the only place where high spirits would be commended rather than vilified. A couple of hours, a lot of alcohol and plenty of barely investigated food later, the entourage lurched back out on to the street, debilitatingly tangled in the quest for fun by the gallon.

Rodney 'Rod the Mod' Bingenheimer was the LA DJ who'd known all the sixties rock legends, had been responsible for first introducing the Sex Pistols to America and first played many of the Creation acts on his K-Rock radio show. He'd been invited along for the ride, but even he seemed to be having trouble keeping up. And this was the man whose LA club, Rodney Bingenheimer's Glam Rock Disco, was the most rock 'n' roll venue on the West Coast in the seventies.

'These guys are wild,' he kept saying. 'Wild.'

'Too fucking right we are,' said Liam. 'Let's have a drink.'

The next stop was the Falcon, a notorious pub venue in Camden, North London constructed by builders who cunningly managed to make it much, much smaller than it looked from the outside, no matter how many times you went. Scottish band Whiteout were playing and Liam decided it would be a great idea to do an unscheduled gig, despite the fact that by this time even standing up had become for everybody more a state of luck than intent. He, Bonehead and Tony got up to lurch their way through a song or two, a slapdash undertaking that even at the time looked a bit of a loopy idea. The bootleg probably sounds like a cat in a blender. The real thing was worse.

Cue the inevitable fist-fight between the brothers Gallagher and a parting of ways that involved everyone present heading off as far as they could go in random directions until they passed out.

'Noel came back to my place,' recalls McGee, 'and he was moaning about Liam for a bit, then we just stayed up all night chopping out and playing records and shouting at each other about our favourite music. He played me this song he'd written, which I think turned out to be "Rockin' Chair" [eventually released as the B-side of 'Roll With It'] and he was going, "So, what do you think?" I was, like, "Look, man, I can't even SEE you, let alone hear what you're playing." It was a pretty good way to celebrate a signing.'

Now they'd finally signed, the band could get down to turning the scores of songs Noel had written into something more tangible. Both Oasis and Creation were keen to restore a confidence and verve to the pop agenda, taking their lead, not altogether surprisingly, from the Beatles and their sixties' peers. Oh, and everything since then while they were at it.

The record business has always been as much about marketing as talent and much of the force behind the Beatles' initial main-stream success came from the way that they and Brian Epstein took note of the way that rock 'n' roll was being sold to its audience, then improved on it.

Back in the early sixties pop was about singles; about 'the Song' as a self-contained entity. Singers and groups often appeared to

be mere conduits for the words and the melody; indeed, particularly in America, they were treated as just that. New York's Brill
Building was packed with songwriters, all working nine to five in
a tiny room with piano, pen and paper, factory-farming classics on
a well-defined, moolah-for-melodies basis. The recording artists
themselves were never allowed to develop personalities that would
subsume the pile-driver force of the Song. Even Elvis Presley, Jerry
Lee Lewis, Little Richard and the other rock 'n' rollers who dared to
be more than all-singing, all-dancing zombies were content to suck
on the security blanket of their master's voice.

In Britain we had Tommy Steele, Cliff Richard and Helen Shapiro.
Walk-on parts in some cheesy pantomime, chirpily prepared to buy
into the notion that careers were for bank clerks and businessmen.
As a 'pop star' you were only there to fill up the space in the 10 x
8 publicity shots. And you never got to keep the negatives. You
did what you were told and if your record company could perhaps
conjure up some sort of fad – 'Hey, kid, we're letting you make
thirteen songs with the word "bop" in the title' – you got to make
an LP. Disposability was an ever-present synonym for success.

The Beatles blew it all away. Not, as is often assumed, because
they stumbled into the arena with any revolutionary desire to
write their own rule book. They were only too keen to tailor
their image according to their manager's brilliantly vicarious construct. Old-school smartness just keeping up appearances. Iconic,
unflinchingly physical sexuality near enough to the surface to
enforce the abandon of the songs. Propriety eternally, seductively
on the verge of flipping into some sort of full-blown, Epicurean
frenzy. Lennon knew. The others just told the tailor their inside-leg
measurements and followed the blueprint of the working-class
escape route that was to generate a thousand copies a minute.
Forever.

Where the Beatles differed from the acts that had come before
them was – and in retrospect it sounds like a passage from *The*

*Book Of The Bleeding Obvious* – that they knew how to write their own songs. Great songs. Loads of them. And they wanted the world to hear them.

Epstein and George Martin both understood the importance of establishing the Beatles primarily as a localized phenomenon aiming at a wider audience, planning to release singles regularly to ensure that their potential audience didn't move on to the next flavour of the month. And, as a by-product, introducing the world to an entirely self-contained pop machine, a signpost for the future.

The Beatles outgrew even their own design. The chronology of their first five singles reveals a definite sense of development, of the band drawing up a life of their own. In the fuss and the bluster, there was an almost imperceptible shift from being passive pop purveyors to actively defining their intentions, exactly what they wanted to be. The bat, not the ball. Their way or nothing.

Taking the Beatles as a starting-point, rock is now forty years old. In the latter half of its teens the vivacious impulse that had been appropriated by John, Paul, George and Ringo and reinforced by the Who, the Rolling Stones, the Small Faces and the rest of the beautiful dreamers had been almost entirely consumed by the monster of self-serving indulgence, obscenely reassured by its complete detachment from the energies that brought it into the world. The Song was forgotten and even the Singer had become just a stepping stone to the difficult, half-hour twiddly bit just after a half-hearted acknowledgement of anything approaching a chorus. If you couldn't handle the lobotomic meanderings of Prog Rock's anaesthetized superstars, you'd have found yourself in the minority, one of the few to hanker still for some sort of edgy, audacious wonder.

I remember other kids at school carrying around a triple album by the Alan Parsons Project, complete with pictures on the sleeve of pyramids and laser beams and grimly impenetrable explanations of the 'concept'. Careless collisions in corridors would see the sleeves unfolding around all and sundry like some sort of dinghy convention. I vowed never to actually listen to one of Parsons's irredeemably overblown records, but I've been told since that they were rather worse than even I had countenanced. But I settled instead for the dopey neo-Nuremberg parp 'n' reverb of ELP's 'Fanfare For The Common Man' and the moment that sums up the seventies above all other, the Eagles' 'Hotel California'. This starts as a lovable, if slightly hippy-dippy account of coke psychosis, before hauling on board a ludicrously obese guitar solo that allows you enough time to go off, make dinner, catch a bit of shut-eye, count the grains of sand in a desert of your choice and tidy up your entire postal district, before it grudgingly resumes its originally intended course. Big, barren and almost entirely boring, it remains rock's Antarctica.

'There's nothing wrong with making eight-minute records,' says Noel. 'You've just got to make it a good eight minutes.'

Just before rock's twentieth birthday, the Sex Pistols came along to piss on the cake. Daring to point fingers at the dinosaurs, the Pistols and the rest of the similarly motivated souls who grouped loosely under the Punk Rock banner wrenched guitar-led music back to sensory slashing. And reintroduced the viability of independent labels, led by Rough Trade, Stiff, Small Wonder and Good Vibrations. Then, in turn, Postcard, Factory and Creation.

'The Sex Pistols are as much of an influence on Oasis as the Beatles,' says Noel. 'And not just 'cos our manager put them on. I always wanted us to have that same kind of "fuck you" attitude. Straight-down-the-line rock music. I've never met them and I'm sure they were complete twats, but I'm sure that's what a lot of people think about us. We don't care either. We just do what they did, make records that fucking blow your head off. There's nothing complicated about what we do. It's not some big intellectual concept or anything. I hate to disappoint people, but there isn't some kind of secret hidden meaning. It's just guitars and words. We're not something you're supposed to think about. All the best records ever made have been cheap-shot stuff. The Beatles were cheap-shot, the Sex Pistols were cheap-shot, the Stone Roses were cheap-shot. "I Wanna Be Adored" isn't about any sort of subtlety, it's just a brilliant "fuck off" song. There's too many bands around now who haven't a clue how to keep things simple. They just want to be fucking hippies. That was what punk was meant to get rid of.'

Punk may have shaken rock as it staggered out of its teenage years, but as it sashayed towards its forties it seemed to have all but forgotten past glories. Save for a few vital signs of life. Independent labels still commanded a vague respect and the post-post-post punk *raison d'être* that had, for a while, collapsed into a deeply dislikeable excuse for smelly no-marks to put records out just for the sad sake of it, found itself reinvigorated by the resolutely anti-corporate (in spirit if not in body) market breech-birthing of the dance scene.

Punk Rock and the Beatles conveniently mark moments where pop music found itself at its purest: songs addressed at an audience who connected instinctively and felt no need for any kind of external justification. Music that was defiantly bewildering to anyone even an inch outside its epicentre. The left side or right side or back bit of the brain, or something, driven entirely by its ability to turn parents conceptually paraplegic. The good stuff.

Creation were always allied with people like Jeff Barrett at Heavenly Records, singularly the most underrated motivator behind the development of 'indiepop' in the past fifteen years and crucial in laying the foundations for the presence of a band like Oasis. It was Barrett who, like Noel, loved both the delicious power of rock and the fresh, extraordinarily purging canopy of Acid House. And, if there's any precedent for Oasis, you have to look to Flowered Up, Heavenly's most important signing. While the Happy Mondays were spending the early nineties whoring their

potential, lugging the Madchester thing towards a shabbily premature demise, Flowered Up were bursting out of a Camden council
estate, naming themselves after the shoots that always manage
to burst through the cracks in the pavement and barging the
proto-funk that the Mondays had snatched from fellow Mancunians
A Certain Ratio towards a definition of modernity ahead of its time.
Songs like 'Egg Rush', 'It's On' and, most importantly, 'Week-
ender' glorified the guitar-dance combustion, paving the way for
Primal Scream's *Screamadelica*, the decade's most influential
genresmashing album. And dug out foundations for Oasis.

'I remember that night when Oasis played "In The City" in
Manchester,' says Jeff Barrett. 'I was down at the University
watching Intastella and when you walked in I started telling you
how great I thought it all was. You just waved your arms about
and kept going on about a band called Oasis and how nothing
else mattered. I was, like, "Yeah, yeah, yeah, the next big thing,
right, tell me about it again when you're sober." First time I saw
them, though, I knew what you meant. Intastella did do a good
gig that night and it seemed like the stuff they were coming out
with [a vaguely affecting, darkly funky take on the Manchester
baggy genre] was the way that the whole Manchester scene was
going to go.

'The baggy thing,' Barrett continues, 'that kind of brought together
a lot of the bands in Manchester and put them into a pigeonhole that
was basically just a music press headline. Manchester's always had
loads of good bands and it's been more about the attitude than the
sound. You listen to records by a load of those groups that were
supposed to be making this new sound and they actually don't
sound a lot like each other. Anyone caught up in all that was
just supposed to be part of some trend and it didn't do anyone
any good.

'I eventually got to hear Oasis, though, and I knew what you'd
been on about. They had a lot in common with Flowered Up in

the way that they obviously loved loud guitars and that whole rock thing. You could see even early on that they had a lot of self-confidence. They knew what they were doing.'

If he'd had a chance, would he have signed them?

'Of course I would. The best thing about them is the way that they're this kind of celebration. Great records are the ones that you just love immediately. You don't need anyone to explain them to you or anything. You're just, like, "Yes!" Gram Parsons did it and the Dexys did it and the Primals and the Chemical Brothers are doing it. Oasis have made people go for great songs again. You can't argue with what they do. Noel writes great songs. That's it.'

The 'great is great' theory has always been a deceptively simplistic code for the Oasis way of doing things. But, like the Beatles long before them, they've always had the ammunition to justify their exuberance, and pinpointed the demonstrative proof behind arrogance as a pop essential. Right from the start they knew what they were doing. And right from the start they knew they were going to do it with the sort of unshatterable confidence that the Beatles had taught them. When John Lennon initiated the dressing-room pep talk, talked about the 'tippermost, toppermost top' as the only destination worth aiming at, he gave Noel Gallagher something to aim at.

'I hate the way that bands go on about how they make records for themselves and if anyone else likes them it's a bonus,' he told Calvin Bush of *Melody Maker* in April 1994.

'Listen, right,' he continued. 'If anybody doesn't buy my music I'm going to be the most upset person in the world. We write music for the guy who walks down the street to get his copy of the fucking *Daily Mirror* and his 20 Bensons every day and he's got fuck all going for him. He's got no money. Even if somebody can't afford to buy our record, if they put on the radio while they're cleaning the house and whistle along and go, "Fucking hell, did you hear that tune?" That's what it's all about.'

Fighting talk, but back at the post-signing dog-end of 1993 the plan to spread the word to the world got snagged on the barbed wire of reality.

Taking a lead from the Beatles, the intent was to put out a single immediately with follow-ups every two months and the release of the debut album as soon as possible. The demo tape and Noel's almost pathological songwriting proclivity suggested that it would be easy.

'It could have been,' says Noel. 'The songs were there and we could have just gone into the studio and knocked them out. There's loads of bands who would have done it and thought, yeah, we've done a great record. We wanted to get it right, though. I knew that we could make a first album that was going to piss on everyone else and I didn't want to just rush out the first thing we did. It had to be the best debut that anyone had ever done and I knew it could be.'

So, while they all stroked their chins and drew up a plan for their first recordings, Oasis continued to play live, lugging their equipment and their attitude through what they call, via the satisfaction of a hell worth wading through, their 'Hamburg Period'. Playing at least three times a week for several months, a discipline that was to contribute to much of their success, they opened for acts as diverse as the Milltown Brothers, Saint Etienne and Liz Phair, sitting rather more comfortably at gigs alongside old friends like Verve and the Real People. Right from the start they'd refused to even think about getting their heads around the role of support band and, while they slogged round the circuit they treated every performance like a headline booking.

'There'd be half a dozen people in the place and half of them would be going off to the bar,' says Noel, 'but we never treated it like, "Well, let's get on, do some songs and then get back to the dressing-room before the main band comes on." Every single time we played I knew that we were the best band on the bill.

We were this great fucking band and we were starting to prove it. Everything was coming together and anyone who went off to the bar was missing out on a band that pissed on the headline acts. Even if there were three people in the audience I'd want to show them that we were worth coming out to see. I mean, we played some fucking brilliant gigs round then and if anyone couldn't be arsed to watch them it's their loss. They're probably telling their mates now that it was the best thing they've ever seen and they spent the whole gig at the bar. Fuck 'em.'

There's a misguided mythology insisting that Oasis never played London until 1994. In fact they'd played several colleges on the outskirts of Dick Whittingtonsville during the previous year, building up a small, crew-cut and not entirely cherishable following among disaffected misfit squaddies in army bases throughout the Home Counties. The first 'proper' London gig, however, took place on 3 November '93 at the Powerhaus in Islington, a much-missed North London venue that featured many of the country's brightest acts teetering on the edge of the big time. In theory, the place attracted a sussed audience that treated it as a consistently rewarding musical showcase rather than just a pub that stayed open late.

Oasis came on stage at the Powerhaus and the audience scuttled back into the shadows, carving out a semicircular berth in front of the stage big enough for a blue whale to flop in and roll about for a bit. The gig had been put on as a showcase for Sony's Dave Massey, just to remind him of what he'd signed and he was suitably impressed by the objects of his deal.

'I started jumping around because every song was a hit,' he remembers. And, as he told *VOX* magazine, 'they had the best eyebrows I've ever seen in my life.'

Alan McGee and I were the only two to venture down the front and I remember reminding myself that no other label boss in the world would ever have been quite so proudly ecstatic as he was.

'They're fucking brilliant,' he declaimed. 'This is the band, Paul. If the Jesus and Mary Chain had been able to play when I first signed them, they'd have been like this. They're just like . . . like . . .'

Lost for words, we both let the cocksure Manc scallies hurl a life-changing manifesto under our arms, through our legs and over our heads to the dunderheads of small talk chatting at tables way back by the wall. Oasis played songs to stun nightingales and deserved far, far more than the polite applause that ushered their departure.

Around then I first realized just how big they could be,' says McGee. 'I remember being on holiday in Hawaii and they sent me out a tape of "Live Forever". I was speechless. It was just this brilliant song that they were sending out so casually, like, "Have a listen to this and tell us what you think." I heard the first few bars of that and I knew just how big they could be. I mean, when I signed them I was thinking they could be big, but I was thinking in terms of the sort of success that Primal Scream or Stone Roses had. There was a feeling that even the most successful band could only get to that kind of level. Or, if they were lucky, they could start to sell on the scale of R.E.M. or someone like that. I heard "Live Forever" and I thought, these really could be the biggest band in the world. A song like that deserves it. It was probably the greatest moment I've ever experienced with them.

'A lot of their success has been up to their management. Marcus and all the people at Ignition have done it exactly right. You can't give Noel enough credit, though. He's 500 times better than any other songwriter around right now, but he's always been that good. Like I say, the first time I heard "Live Forever" I knew we'd signed something really special. I was sitting in Hawaii listening to it and thinking, fuck, this is really going to be big.'

As one of the few people to dare to snap the taboo on any band being as big, if not bigger than, the Beatles, I wasn't altogether surprised to find colleagues and even people close to the band wary of agreeing that Oasis had the potential to redraw rock's boundaries.

'The Beatles were there as this benchmark,' says McGee, 'and they were outside any kind of competition. I wanted everyone else to get into Oasis like I had the first time I saw them play. That was as much as I expected. It's brilliant to see the success they're getting now and no one deserves it as much as Noel, but it's gone way beyond what I'd ever thought.'

'I always said we'd be the biggest band in the world,' says Noel. 'When we started, of course, we were telling everyone we were going to do this and do that. We had to give it all that bullshit. These days, though, I know that I can write better songs than anyone else around. Our kid's the best singer and the gigs are a million miles better than anyone else. We've worked for it all, though. I mean, even when we first signed to Creation we were all skint. I remember my twenty-seventh birthday. I'd been kicked out of my flat and I was in this tiny hotel room, phone off the hook, really pissed off. We've not just been lying around waiting for the cheques to come in. We've worked hard to get where we are 'cos we knew what we could do.'

# 4

## LIVE IN THE STUDIO

Back in late '93 Oasis may well have known what they could do, but, to anyone who hadn't yet seen them live, they were still trading on nothing more than mouthy self-confidence. It was time for something more solid.

'The first single was obviously going to be really important,' says Creation's Johnny Hopkins. 'Noel had always said that he wanted the band to put out a single every three months, just like the Beatles. With most people there'd be an obvious song that stood out, something so you could go, "Yeah, that's the single" or whatever. The thing with Oasis, though, was that they always had so many brilliant things written, right from the start. I mean, every week you'd hear a load of new stuff and there'd be, like, ten songs that could easily be a single.'

'Right now I think I can write really good songs,' says Noel. 'Back when we first signed I knew that our stuff was pretty fucking top. That was three years ago and I look at a lot of it now and think, well, I can do better than that now. But compared to anything else around at the time, it was all right. We were doing fast, punky songs and it was a real in-your-face sound, but all the other bands that the music press were writing about were poncing about trying to be clever, getting into something that didn't have any tunes or anything. We've never pretended we wanted to be fashionable or arty or anything. The thing about Oasis songs is that they're really direct. They don't fuck about. If you want some kind of weird, twiddly stuff then go ahead, listen to someone else. Our records are just fucking rock 'n' roll songs. And in twenty years' time everyone's going to remember us, not some indie band making a noise.'

'Every single Oasis song is a classic,' says Liam. 'If I just, like, dropped dead, those songs would always be there and I'd have been singing them. Our kid writes things that I sing and if I didn't like them I'd tell him. I have before. Even when we were going to gigs supporting a load of twats I knew we were better than them. It's the fucking songs and the singer, mate. We just pissed on them. Always will.'

So has it always been about self-confidence?

'No, it's always been about being fucking better than anyone else.'

'Oasis put music back by years,' says Billy Greeves from Fire Records, the label that signed Pulp a decade before the Britpop hoo-ha. Greeves is, with reservations, an Oasis fan, but voices a bravely perceptive theory.

'They were just like the Beatles in that they put music back by years,' he says. 'When the Beatles started they were accused of being retro and that's exactly what they were. They were making records that were directly influenced by things that had happened five years earlier. Buddy Holly and Chuck Berry and all that. So it took a lot of the attention away from the way that British music was starting to develop through the easy-listening, jazz stuff and genuinely original producers like Joe Meek.

'And when Oasis came out,' he continues, 'they were doing all that Beatles stuff and making records that sounded really

46

obviously like everything from the Beatles through the Smiths to the Stone Roses and all that "baggy" scene. They made indie rock mainstream and suddenly if you were on an independent label you had to start writing pop songs.

'The Beatles put British rock back by five years,' he repeats. 'So did Oasis. I like their records, but I wonder what would have happened if they'd never existed.'

It was the sort of worst-case scenario that even some of us close to the band were beginning to think about considering once they made it clear that they weren't going to put out a debut record until well into 1994.

Looking back, it was a daringly confident move, but at the time it seemed like a 'fuck-you new future' was going to peter out into some sort of elaborately wasted opportunity.

'We always knew what we were doing,' says Tim Abbot, another important player in the Oasis story. At the time they signed he was in charge of marketing at Creation and, although he has since left to concentrate on his own record label, Better, and a management company that looks after ex-Take That man Robbie Williams among others, he remains a confidant, friend and adviser to the band.

'They had loads of songs,' says Abbot, 'but they wanted anything they put out to be great. It had to be just right. There wasn't going to be any point in putting out an Oasis record that was just going to be half-arsed. Everyone who'd heard them or seen them live knew that they weren't some chancers coming along trying to get in the papers or anything. They were fucking brilliant and anyone who'd been to one of their gigs was going to know that. They could have just gone in a studio, recorded something quick and put it out, but it was never as desperate as that. It was always about quality.'

Instead, as Oasis continued to gig around the country, Creation took the song 'Columbia' from the original demo and pressed up 510 copies (playfully insisting at the time that they'd only done sixty and that the artefact was even more of a collector's item). Copies were placed in selected crevices in the media cliff face in November and December of 1993 and the record found itself on Radio 1's playlist. It was the first time that any label had managed to chisel a song by a freshly signed group on to national radio – a song that was never going to be released as a single and which triumphantly bore the ragged edges of its still semi-defined status.

'Once word got out, everyone was killing each other to get a copy,' says Abbot.

The song itself was a perfect introduction to Oasis's reason for not sitting at home and shutting up. Tidal-wave guitars drenched a melody that almost recalled the Happy Mondays and the Stone Roses, the Liam drawl tightrope-talking the knowingly innocent couplet 'I can't tell you the way I feel/'Cos the way I feel is oh so new to me', the whole managing to sound both like something you'd heard a hundred times before and something sparklingly, brutally new. It got played on the radio. A lot.

'It was great to sit down and hear a song I'd written on the radio,' says Noel, 'and I thought, well, whatever happens, I did that, but I knew they'd be playing loads more. "Columbia" wasn't the best song we had, even then.'

The conception of 'Columbia' remains a darned good starting-point for an argument among anyone within a hundred yards of Oasis during their early years. Liam claims he wrote at least a verse, and the Real People mention in passing that they might have contributed. Noel gets the publishing royalties. No one starts tugging lawyers into it all. Churlish never lasts till morning.

Radio play for 'Columbia' ensured a few more people down the front at Oasis's support slots during the last few months of '93 and early '94, the band, for a while at least, content to do the pinball thing up and down the motorways of the nation.

'There were loads of gigs at really small venues,' says Guigs, 'but we all knew it was going to go on to something bigger.'

'It's what you do,' says Bonehead. 'You go somewhere, play about five minutes after the doors have opened to ten people, then pack up and go home.'

'I was mad for it,' says Liam. 'If the crowd had come along for someone else then they missed out on us. The ones that were into us had a good time. Good luck to them. They were into it.'

'Most of the people we supported were terrible,' says Noel. 'You go, "What are we doing supporting you?" But then you think, well, you'll be supporting us in a year's time. We're doing gigs for 20,000 people now and there's platinum discs in the hall. They're still playing pubs. Hey, I think we were the ones who knew what we were doing, right?'

Well, no, not if you'd belly-flopped into Oasis's early studio forays for Creation.

'The plan was for them to do a new version of "Bring It On Down" as the first single,' says Johnny Hopkins. 'It was the most obvious one off the tape to put out, so they went to do that and start on the album.'

First choice as producer was one Dave Batchelor, who'd worked with the Sensational Alex Harvey Band and the Skids. Noel had worked with him at Inspiral Carpets gigs and promised him, characteristically impulsively, a chance to oversee their first recordings.

'Noel and Tim Abbot and Marcus would come along to my flat in Rotherhithe with all these tapes,' says Alan McGee, 'and they'd sit there all night playing them. To be honest, I was on a different planet back then and even if they'd been bringing along the greatest tapes in the world I'd have been too fucked up to notice. I'm really grateful that they had so much patience.'

The band themselves were beginning to run out of patience with the idea of Batchelor as producer.

'The songs they came out with were obviously, even to me back then, not nearly as good as the demos,' recalls McGee. 'The thing is that when Oasis had done one of those original demos they'd gone into the studio and basically just done the songs live. They'd record everything as a band and then do guitar and vocal bits over the top at the end if they needed to. It was the most simple way you could record anything and they'd done it because that was the way they had to.

'With Dave Batchelor they were doing it all completely differently. There was this big multi-track studio and he obviously thought, well, let's do everything separately. So they'd do each bit on its own and then mix it all at the end. And it didn't sound the same. I'd seen them live and I'd heard a tape that was basically done like a live performance. There was something missing with the stuff that Dave Batchelor was doing and the way that he was doing it.'

'Dave Batchelor was really old,' says Noel, 'and he'd been through all these years in the business, so he had really set ideas about how you should do things. I'd come along to the studio, get pissed, then say, "Tell you what, let's compress this to fuck so the speakers blow up." I wanted the Oasis sound to be, like, this huge roar. He'd go, "Oh, no, you can't do that, that's not the way we do it, we never have done." He was trying to be really sensible about everything while I was more interested in just going with this mad, fucking noise. I wanted it to be louder than any record ever made. And eventually I just thought, hey, this is my fucking band, not his. So it was obvious he was going to have to go.'

'I remember sitting round in a studio somewhere for hours,' says Johnny Hopkins. 'We literally spent a whole night listening to all these versions of "Bring It On Down" and each one was supposed to be different. By the end of the night, though, they'd all blurred into one. I think it was Alan who got it right when he said, "Well, it's not that any of them are more right than any of the others. They're all wrong." We'd all got so close to the whole thing that we'd almost forgotten why we liked it in the first place. You'd take a step back, though, and you'd realize it just didn't have that kind of energy that the demo and the live gigs had. It should have been better.'

They let Dave Batchelor go. A girl call Anjali Dutt, who'd worked on some of the My Bloody Valentine stuff for Creation, was brought in to help with the engineering. Noel suggested Mark Coyle as producer. Coyle was already the band's sound man at gigs and had an instinctive ability to turn their self-perception into a concrete reality. It seemed that if anyone was going to be able to transfer the band's strength to any kind of permanent testament, it was going to be him. He knew what they were SUPPOSED to sound like. And Noel was insistent that they go back to their old way of recording, 'live' performance in the studio acting as the skeleton on which to hang guitars and vocals.

The Batchelor sessions may well have been largely dumped in the trash can marked 'Start All Over Again', but they did throw up one song that was to make it on to the eventual version of the band's first album. 'Slide Away' was for a long time the greatest, most personal song that Noel had ever written, a glorious, lovelorn anthem for both the demolition of the romantic ideal and the eternal spark of hope. The eagle struggling across continents with a broken wing.

Days after a rough version of the song had been recorded, Noel gave me a tape. Splitting up with a girlfriend at the time, I listened to it every night in the darkness. Lost, lonely tears silently counting out the things I should have said. Words that still bring up bruises, a sound that remains both suicide and salvation. That it was, and will for ever be, a distant cousin of the Style Council's 'You're The Best Thing' only confirms its rug-pulling, disorientatingly impressive force. The very first suggestion that Oasis were going to do more than just molest you with incessantly obvious melodies.

'Slide Away' was mixed by Owen Morris, a Welsh visionary who happened to be engineering at one of the many studios Oasis were to pile into between November 1993 and much of the first half of '94.

'When we did that song,' he says, 'everyone was off their heads. I just turned everything up and it meant it all got distorted. It wasn't like I thought, oh yeah, this is going to be an Oasis sound.'

Morris was, however, to become an integral part of just that 'Oasis sound' even if its existence had not yet been admitted. Coyle was to produce much of the early stuff, but Morris later developed an unspoken interpretation of a contemporary 'Wall of Sound'. These days he's almost the sixth member of Oasis, an essential accompaniment to Noel's creativity.

'He writes the songs and he says, "I want it to sound like this,"' Morris explains. 'He's got this idea in his head of what it's all going to sound like. I turn the knobs and all that, but they're his songs. Everyone wants to come along and write about arguments and things, but Oasis record really quickly.'

Not in '93, they didn't. The band were shuttled around studios all over Britain, stumbling towards some way of finding how to mould their force on record. Monnow Valley, in Wales, was at least to yield a cover shoot for the sleeve of their first single and a notable meeting between the Stone Roses and the heirs to their crown.

'We were in Monmouth,' says Noel. 'It's not far from Monnow Valley and we'd gone off to do some shopping. We were walking down the road and suddenly Ian Brown from the Roses came out of WH Smith. He goes, "You're those guys from Oasis, right?" And we're, like, "Yeah, have you heard of us then?" He goes, "Course I have. It's about time someone like you came along." This was one of the people who'd made me want to write songs and here he was saying he liked our band. It was great.'

Having made contact, Oasis and the Stone Roses soon nurtured their relationship through some intense partying, made all the more convenient by the fact that Brown and his band were based at the nearby Rockfield studios, working on apparently never-ending sessions for their *Second Coming* album.

Johnny Hopkins remembers one particularly wild night.

'We were staying in a room above a pub a few miles from the studios and everyone had been partying all night. I eventually got back to bed and a few hours later I heard someone throwing stones at the window. I looked out and there was Mani from the Roses. Behind him, going off into the distance there were these tracks just going across fields as far as you could see. He'd nicked a tractor and just pointed it straight at where we were staying. He went, "All right? Where's the party then?" It was mad.'

The partying may have been coming along nicely, but the recording was far less fruitful. Over the period of a few months Oasis were booked into a heap of studios: Monnow Valley, Rockfield and Loco in Wales, Olympic Studio in Barnes, Matrix in Fulham, Sawmills in Cornwall and the Pink Museum in Liverpool. It seemed that their almost pathological propensity for touring was being replicated even without an audience present.

Some of the sessions threw up little more than curiously tangential bootleg fodder like Noel filling a whole tape with cover versions of Rolling Stones songs. At the Pink Museum, however, they went in ostensibly to record some prospective B-sides for their first single and ended up writing and recording a whole new A-side, a song called 'Supersonic'.

As debuts go, it's up there with the best and a supreme introduction to a band who admitted to assimilating all the finest rock moments from the past thirty years. As the guitar cascade echoes the Sex Pistols' 'Pretty Vacant' in comes a compacted appropriation of everything from the Who, the Stones and the Beatles, through the jagged cacophony of punk and the rhythmic swathe of the Stone Roses. And, at its heart, something brand-new, something of their own. The opening lines, 'I'm feeling supersonic/Give me gin and tonic', perfectly anticipate the mixture of arrogance, elation and playfulness that define much of Oasis's work. It's the Big Bang around which their universe continues to expand.

Lyrically the song demonstrated a determination to put style and spirit over content, Noel confessing that the words were just nonsense. And so, while people stroked their chins and wondered what kind of grim drug shenanigans could be behind a couplet that went 'I know a girl called Elsa/She's into Alka Seltzer', Noel stayed quiet, knowing that it was merely inspired by a Rottweiler of that name running around the studio when the song was written.

Before the release of their single, the band continued to tour, picking up a curmudgeonly review from *NME* and ensuring that the writer, Johnny Cigarettes, went straight to the top of the band's hate list. That one hiccup apart, the band's self-confidence was soaring. The first signs that they intended to bring their scally roots with them came after a low-key gig in Gleneagles when they drank the bar dry and stole a whole load of motorized lawnmowers to make their escape, dementedly mowing their way into the distance. It was the kind of gloriously dumb gesture that was to mark out much of their early existence and guaranteed plenty of column inches, first in the music press and then, as a sign of real success, in the tabloids.

First though, they set about convincing any remaining cynics in the London musical village with a gig at the Water Rats in King's Cross on 27 January. An invite-only affair, it filled the tiny pub, with 200 people left outside. Inside was hotter than any sauna and anyone more than ten feet from the tiny stage was to catch only the occasional glimpse of the band everyone had been talking about. The sound, however, left no one in any doubt that Oasis were something very, very special, a loud, uncompromisingly straightforward argument for reconsidering the force of guitar music. While they were in no way a dance band, Oasis seemed to have captured much of the dynamism of that genre, conveying instinctively a sense of millennial apocalypse.

They'd come not only to breathe new life into rock, but first to destroy their peers.

It was a short set, but the quality of the songs took away what breath hadn't already been forced out by the heat and the crush. Bruised and dizzy, the disciples squeezed out into the night knowing things would never be quite the same.

Afterwards the atmosphere in the dressing-room was, not surprisingly, ecstatic. The cool self-confidence that would stud interviews over the next few months had been put aside as the band realized that they'd come through their first major trial, they'd made their point and they could get on with being even better. Back at their hotel, they drank with Olympian gusto and buzzed as much on adrenalin as any artificial stimulants.

A couple of weeks later they found themselves in the news after an attempt to play a gig in Amsterdam, their first overseas performance.

Johnny Hopkins explained to Radio 1 what had happened.

'What happened was, they were on this ferry going over from Harwich overnight and they'd all got pissed up. There was some big fight and Liam and Guigs got blamed for it and got locked up in the bottom of the boat. While all this was happening, Tony and Noel and Bonehead must have been asleep. There was another group of lads in the corridor over from them and there'd been a bit of banter between them. What must have happened was that when Bonehead was asleep they'd broken into his room and stolen all his clothes. He woke up at some point and realized what was going on, so he ran up and down the corridor knocking on all the doors. So he got carted off. Tony stuck his head round the door to see what was happening and that was him gone as well. Noel woke up the next morning and he's, like, "Where's me band?" and he's told, "Well, they're all in the cells."'

Liam, Bonehead, Guigs and Tony all ended up going straight back to England on the same boat they'd come out on. They never even got on foreign soil. Noel mooched around Amsterdam for a couple of days, musing on what might have been.

While the four members of the band who'd been arrested appeared at the time to be proud of what they considered great rock 'n' roll behaviour, Noel was inclined to agree with Marcus's view of the situation.

'You think that was rock 'n' roll,' he'd said. 'That's not rock 'n' roll. What IS rock 'n' roll is going over to Amsterdam, playing a great gig and blowing people away. Not getting thrown off some ferry like football hooligans.'

That kind of level-headedness was to come in increasingly useful as the band set about fully living up to their bad-boy image. Apart from the incident with the lawnmowers in Gleneagles and the ferry arrests, they'd also been caught climbing into Stonehenge to reclaim it for the people and, during a show in Southampton, Noel had punched Liam in the face and chased him all the way back to the dressing-room.

'We were just getting used to it all then,' says Noel. 'At least we were more interesting than any of the other fuckers around.'

Somewhere in all the chaos they finally got their recording sessions for the album together and recorded the whole thing in a ten-day spurt at the Sawmills Studio in Cornwall. Well away from any opportunity for misbehaviour, they were forced into channelling their energies into work. It was the spur they needed. And, having got the album out of the way, they could concentrate on having more fun.

In March they made their first TV performance, on *The Word*, giving a taster of 'Supersonic', which was to be released the next month. Waving around a video camera, they seemed at once a captivating object of attention and something scarier, more controlling. You got the feeling that they knew you couldn't stop staring at them and that they were staring right back, waiting, planning. Getting ready.

'Supersonic' was released in April and went to number thirty-one in the charts. It had started.

To trumpet the release of the single, the band spent most of March on a three-week tour with Whiteout, the band who'd played the Falcon on the night of the Sony signing. Original plans were for the bands to alternate headlining slots, but after only a few dates it became obvious that Oasis would have to headline each night. Whiteout were starting to get sick of being blown offstage before they themselves had even got out of the dressing-room. And while Oasis were only picking up about £100 a night, they managed to fuel enough mayhem to ensure that they were banned from several hotels.

The climax of the tour came with a gig at the 100 Club in Oxford Street, the site of a legendary Pistols show and a place that had played host to many more great performers during the sixties and seventies. Oasis again played a blistering show and while they fully demonstrated their aptitude for hardly moving on stage, their stillness began to make perfect sense. Such was the splendour of their noise that any hint of crowd-pleasing showmanship would have demeaned its hypnotic appeal. They were beginning to sound unstoppable. Not that the Metropolitan Police thought so. They pulled the band on the way from the gig to the hotel because they thought they looked like they were up to something, only letting them go when copies of the single were waved around.

What they should have realized was that Oasis always looked like they were up to something, acting more and more like outriders for some Care in the Community programme. The arguments on stage continued and, as interviewees, the Liam and Noel double act proved as fearsome as waking up in the middle of the night and finding yourself refereeing a heavyweight championship bout. And when the Gallaghers started arguing you'd have to be stupid to even try to pull them apart.

Things came to a head in an *NME* interview in April when

journalist John Harris met up with them in Glasgow's Forte Crest Hotel. Halfway through the interview Liam and Noel suddenly turned on each other and started an argument that went on for the best part of the next hour. It was a masterpiece in pointless thrust and counter-thrust, taking on a life of its own and evolving into something only distantly related to reality. Sections of it were later released as a single on Fierce Panda records under the banner 'Wibbling Rivalry' and it's almost as entertaining as their songs themselves.

Take this, for example:

LIAM: You want to be Andrew Lloyd Webber, you do, you fucker.

NOEL: Who's Andrew Lloyd Webber?

LIAM: I haven't got a clue. He's a golfer or something.

Or how about this?

NOEL: You like shagging loads of whores.

LIAM: Yeah, I do. Look, all I've got to say is, I'm just having a crack. It's not doing anyone any harm. John Lennon used to do loads of mad things . . .

NOEL: Do you know John Lennon?

LIAM: Yeah, I do.

NOEL: Well you must be pretty old then. How old are you? Twenty-one?

LIAM: No, about 1005.

NOEL: You're twenty-two and I watched you being born, so shut the fuck up about knowing John Lennon.

LIAM: I'm not a pop star. And if I am I'm a real one, matey. I haven't been invented. I'm an average lad who was born in Burnage, who played conkers . . .

NOEL: CONKERS!!!

LIAM: Conkers, mate. Conkers. The fucking lot. Conkers. That is it. And now I'm in a band and nothing's fucking changed. I'm not an idol. I'm not a faker. I'm not some fucking bullshitter, I just say what I say.

From then on Noel and Liam avoided doing interviews together. Probably for the best.

Another *NME* journalist, Simon Williams, hooked up with them in early May and found them in admirably unhinged form.

At a hotel in Portsmouth they managed to fill a swimming pool with chairs, steal several hundred quids' worth of booze, get into a fight with half the other residents, flirt with every girl in the building and still managed to get up in time for their breakfast of cigarettes, Jack Daniels, gin and tonics and the odd Big Mac. Looking back at their behaviour the next day, Liam had noted, 'Well, it was a silly place to put a swimming pool, wasn't it?,' Noel adding, 'Yeah and those plate-glass windows were just saying, "Throw a chair through me!"'

The next night the King's Hotel in Newport received similar treatment (even though it had a bar called the Oasis) and Bonehead was rapidly establishing himself as a man with a mission to trash anywhere that he found himself in for more than thirty seconds.

'I remember we were stuck in the tour bus in a traffic jam,' says Williams, 'and Bonehead decided to leap from the front to the back seat. And he was supposed to be driving.'

Noel summed up the mood of the moment.

'People go on about the pressure of touring and all that, but that's because they sit and think about it all day. But we'll just bowl up there arguing in the coach all the way. Someone will probably have a tooth missing by the time we get on stage and we'll play the gig and then we'll get off and start arguing again. With this band it's let your hair down, man, have a good time. That's what it's there for. Then you wake up in the morning and do it all over again.'

They were still young, still getting the first giddy rush of fame. And they could get up the next morning and do it all over again. Alan McGee wasn't so sure that he could.

'I'd been doing it for years and it was just getting more and more mad. I was starting to fall apart, both physically and mentally, and

I knew if I didn't stop I was going to die. So I went into a detox clinic. By that time I'd completely lost it and it took me a long time to recover. It took me the best part of a year to recover and yeah, I regret not being there to see the band really take off, but I don't for a minute regret getting myself together and cleaning up. I thought that Noel would be really dismissive of me, but out of almost everyone he was the one who seemed to be able to accept it the easiest. I think it brought me and him a lot closer.'

And so, while McGee took a much-needed sabbatical on the sidelines, the band prepared for some of the busiest months of their career. Creation had organized an 'Undrugged' night at the Albert Hall to celebrate ten years in business. The name was both a nod to the queue of stars ready to appear on MTV's *Unplugged* slot and also perhaps a quiet acknowledgement of McGee's long journey to recovery. Oasis were scheduled to appear at the show and a couple of weeks beforehand they attended a press conference to publicize the event. Afterwards they headed off to Camden's Good Mixer pub, a notorious indie-pop hang-out. It was there that the first seeds of the rivalry between Oasis and Blur were to be sown. While Liam and Blur's guitarist Graham alternated between bonhomie and animosity (the equation for their relationship drawn up by a complex formula involving how much drink had been consumed and who was holding the drugs), Noel took an immediate dislike to singer Damon Albarn.

'I remember I said to him, "Go on, get the drinks in, you're rich" and he got all funny about it, saying that we were just, like, shit Northerners, poncing off him. I just thought, well, fuck you then, mate. I mean, he's always been a twat.'

Later on that evening, at Camden Underworld, Liam continued to bait the band and ended up getting a, some might say, deserved kicking from one of their entourage.

'If I act like a dick then someone should give me a slap,' Liam told me a couple of months later. 'That's all right if they want to do that. I don't like it when people bottle it up, though, and say all these snide things behind my back. If they say it to my face, fair enough. They might be right and I might be right, but at least it's out in the open. That's the way it should be.'

By now Oasis had even started a singsong on their bus to the tune of the Small Faces' 'Lazy Sunday'. It went, 'Wouldn't it be nice to be a fucking cockney/Wouldn't it be nice to be in fucking Blur.' Not perhaps Noel's greatest lyric to date, but it presages the genuine mutual dislike that was to follow a year later.

A couple of warm-up gigs were scheduled before the Albert Hall show, in Windsor and Ilford. At the second, the night before Undrugged, the band's performance was constantly disrupted by dorky stage-divers completely failing to comprehend the transfixing nature of the band's music, a daft minority of the audience happier to lob themselves off-stage like they were at some crusty playschool.

'I've never understood stage-diving,' says Liam. 'I mean, what's the point? Especially when we're playing. You wouldn't have stage-dived to the Beatles, right? So don't stage-dive to us, you cheeky bastards.'

Liam sat at the back of the stage for much of the gig, increasingly pissed off at what he and the rest of the band considered an invasion of their personal space. To this day they are one of the few bands, particularly in America, who insist on barriers between themselves and the crowd.

'If people want to get on stage,' says Noel, 'then why don't they form a band or something? Don't come dicking around with us.'

The last straw at Ilford came when someone grabbed Liam's cherished star-shaped tambourine out of his hand and made off with it. The band stopped mid-song and walked off the stage.

Next day, still pissed off, Liam decided not to play at the Undrugged night. It was left to Bonehead and Noel to do a short set comprising their single 'Shakermaker', 'Live Forever' and a fledgeling version of 'Whatever', still known at that time as 'Whatever I'.

Noel met Paul McCartney recently and mused on how awful it must have been for McCartney never to have seen the Beatles live, never to have gone out front and watched the greatest band in the world at the time. He continued that it was the only bad thing about being in Oasis. He never got to see them.

Liam felt much the same, but that night at the Albert Hall he got the chance. And despite the good-natured heckles that he hurled at Noel from next to me in the box, at the end of the show he turned and said, 'That was fucking brilliant. I'm proud of him.' It is one of the few times I've heard him expressly articulate any tenderness towards his brother, even if it's always just beneath the surface.

Afterwards Noel admitted that he was nervous, but had enjoyed the buzz, jokingly saying to Liam, 'I don't need you any more.' In fact the performance paved the way for the 'solo Noel bit' that is now a regular part of any Oasis show.

In June, Oasis released 'Shakermaker', one of their older songs, which had been written forty-eight hours before their 1993 'In The City' show. While the lyrics were ostensibly more 'I Am The Walrus'-type gibberish, they in fact drew on many of the formative touchstones in Noel's youth, from kids' TV, the Jam, distantly remembered adverts and even a nod to the guy who sold him his first records at Mr Sifter's. Of rather more concern was the idea of lifting an entire couplet from an old Coca-Cola advert and, fearing litigation from the multinational, a few lyric changes were made for the recorded version. Threats of legal action from the New Seekers (whose 'I'd Like To Teach The World To Sing' provided the basis for the Coke ad) never materialized, but Noel actually seemed more pissed off that he wasn't being sued by Paul McCartney.

'No one seems to notice that it sounds like "Flying" by the Beatles,' he said. 'If I'm going to be sued by anyone it's going to be by the best.'

It wasn't to be the last time that Noel's unabashed filching of 'the best bits' from tunes he liked was to get the lawyers hovering.

In many ways 'Shakermaker' was, however, different from other Oasis songs of the time. While the band always closed shows with their version of 'I Am The Walrus', the songs rarely indulged such oblique meanderings. Noel's lyrical strength came from his directness, his ability to communicate the upliftingly anthemic. Still, when he appeared on Channel 4's *Naked City*, you could have been forgiven for thinking that he'd turned into an acid head.

In the middle of an interview with the show's host he suddenly stopped dead.

'Look at that butterfly,' he nodded. Was he tripping?

'I really did see a butterfly,' he told me later. 'I don't know how the fuck it got into the studio, but it did. I mean, I wasn't sober, but when I get pissed I don't start seeing butterflies flying around. Know what I mean? I've never been into that psychedelic business.'

The single got to number eleven, giving the band their first *Top Of The Pops* appearance; it was a ritual that was soon to assume a glorious regularity.

'The first time was good,' says Liam. 'You see It on the telly when you're young and then suddenly you're on it. It's weird.'

Noel achieved another of his ambitions the night after the *Naked City* performance. Ian McNabb, ex-singer with the Icicle Works, was playing King's College, London with Ralph Molina and Billy Talbot of Crazy Horse and Noel, a long-time Neil Young fan, was invited up to join in on the encore, a cover of the Seeds' 'Pushin' Too Hard'.

'They said, "Do you know how it goes?"' he recalls, 'and I went, "Oh yeah, sure," even though I only vaguely knew it. Anyway, afterwards in the dressing-room, one of them comes up to me and he says, "Hey, little man, you really can play." Them saying that to me was a top moment.'

Liam was less impressed.

'What the fuck did he want to play with those old farts for?' he asked a few days later. 'I mean, he's got his own songs and his own band and all he wants to do is play with a bunch of sixty-year-olds. He's weird.'

Not half as weird as the whole band were to be a few days later when they played their first festival: Glastonbury.

'It was never the sort of place I'd ever felt even the slightest desire to go to,' says Noel. 'The only reason we went was because we were playing, but we thought, well, if we're there we might as well have a good time.'

They didn't just have a good time: they disembowelled the concept, roasted it on an open fire and spread the bones over a hundred-mile radius.

'It was completely mad,' recalls Simon, a friend of theirs whom they knew as 'the Cat in the Hat'. He'd brought along a big bag of E's and enough bindles of coke to ensure that the band were able to plunge wholeheartedly into the Glastonbury Experience. And within seconds of their arrival it became obvious that they intended to do just that.

'I was standing in this field,' recalls Simon, 'and this van came along and almost ran me over. Out jumped the band and all their mates and they just started necking all the stuff like it was going to run out any minute. They were bombing about all over the place, wandering off miles away from where they were supposed to be playing. About five minutes before they were supposed to go on someone found them and dragged them to their stage and they just went on and played this phenomenal gig. If you'd seen them beforehand you wouldn't have thought they'd even have been able to stand up. When they came off they just started going for it again on a big mad one. I think Liam even slept in a tent, but I haven't a clue how he managed to put it up.'

The next night, back in London, they still hadn't stopped partying. Booked in at the notorious rock 'n' roll haunt, the Columbia Hotel in

Bayswater Road (a place memorably described by Liam as looking like 'the sort of place your granny would stay'), they ended the night throwing bottles out of a window at a Mercedes in the car park. Unfortunately, the car belonged to the hotel manager and they found themselves only the third group ever to be banned from the place.

'It was a shit place anyway,' says Liam. 'We've been thrown out of a lot nicer places.'

I wonder how their working-class upbringing and the sense of respect that their mother instilled in them when they were young tallies with such relentlessly antisocial behaviour.

'We're lads,' they said at the time.

Nowadays, though, Noel is more circumspect.

'We smashed up hotels because basically it was a laugh and it's something that just kind of happens when you're all running around with this mad energy. And we did end up having to pay for it all. At one point it was getting completely bonkers. I'd be doing interviews with my back to the window and the journalist would be looking over my shoulder open-mouthed when I was saying that it was all just rumours about us trashing hotels. I'd be saying that and she'd be seeing all these things dropping past the window behind me. Beds, wardrobes, everything. I did make sure my room never got trashed, though, if I could help it. I mean, call me old-fashioned, but I like to have a bed to sleep in at the end of the night.

'Anyway, we don't do that now,' Noel adds. 'We just had to get it out of our system and I'm glad we did. Everyone ought to do it once, just to see what it feels like.'

The mood suitably euphoric, there was only one thing to do, one place to go. Time to take Manhattan.

# 5

## TAKING AMERICA

It was 21 July 1994 and Liam looked out of the window of his room at New York's Paramount Hotel. 'Tonight,' he said, staring at the bright light, big-city skyline, 'you're mine.' While the band's British and European ascendancy had been achieved with almost unbelievable ease, America was always going to be far more of a problem. Relatively unknown Stateside, they were also almost completely at odds with the all-consuming grunge genre with which Young America was fixated. Pearl Jam topped the charts and the recent death of Kurt Cobain had fuelled Nirvana's popularity saleswise. Five scallies from Manchester might have liked to give the impression that the Americans were just going to roll over and give them all their money, but even they knew it wasn't going to be quite so easy.

'Everything was going so fast for us back then in Britain,' recalls Noel. 'It was just getting unreal. So I think we went over with this cocky attitude that we could do anything and that we didn't much care about making it in America anyway. I've still got some of that feeling. It's such a mad, huge country. You have to tour for months before people even know you're there. Of course, now, it's a lot easier for us and we're selling loads of records in America, playing big gigs, but back then we were just these snotty kids coming along telling the Americans we had the best songs they were ever going to hear. We were right, obviously, but it just took them a while to cotton on.'

And so, on 19 July 1994, Oasis found themselves in New York on the back of the New Music Seminar, an annual music-biz beano that exists purely to provide executives from around the world with an opportunity to bump up their expenses claims and trot out dreary, soulless plans for corporate unit-shifting. And while British bands like These Animal Men and Echobelly paraded under the 'official' Seminar banner, Oasis remained defiantly distanced from it all.

'We're not part of all this,' Noel told me. 'We're far more important than some stupid industry circus.'

The night before, executives from Sony had taken the band out for a meal. Halfway through dinner they told Liam that he should be grateful to be on such an important label. He stood up, told them it was the other way round and they could all go fuck themselves. And left.

'Those American companies are mostly run by idiots,' says Noel. 'When we were first looking for a label to sign with out there, we got someone to take a tape out. The guy listened to it in his office and said, "Hey, you guys are from Manchester, right? Well, you don't sound much like Jesus Jones, do you?" Our mate just pressed the eject button, took the tape out and got the next flight home. I mean, you're dealing with complete twats. And I'm sure there's loads of bands who would have gone for the first person they met just because they were American. We weren't about to sell ourselves so cheap.'

Instead they spent much of their time on their first American visit adopting a kind of swaggering bunker mentality. On the night

I arrived we all decamped straight to their hotel bar, along with half a dozen new mates that they'd picked up on a drinking spree the night before. Relentlessly taking the piss out of a barman by telling him he was the dead spit of Ryan Giggs (to a not surprisingly blank response), they proceeded to run up an $800 tab in little over an hour. And Noel told me about the music that had inspired him, the people he wanted not just to equal but to better.

'The Beatles, the Pistols, the Who, Neil Young, the Stone Roses, even things like the Bee Gees. I always thought they were a load of old shite, but then someone gave me a tape of their early stuff and it's brilliant. There's so much music, so many great bands, and I want to hear them all. I know we can be as good as any of them, but you've got to check out the competition, haven't you? The only bands I don't understand are the Clash and the Beach Boys. I just don't get what people see in them.'

Any other misconceptions?

'Well, until six months ago, I thought Blondie were French.'

The following night, before the gig, Liam sat in my room, laid into the Class A's and told me how a few months earlier he'd slept with an older woman, a barmaid at his local pub, and how he'd been worried he might have caught something. Then he realized that he couldn't have, that he'd been worrying just for the sake of it.

'I want something better than all that,' he explained to me. 'That whole life of going down the pub, copping off, living that boring, fucking way. I want to do something great, something that's just going to fuck off everyone I ever knew. Something that's going to blow them away. That's why I love being in this band, man. It's doing something that everyone's going to remember for ever. We're going to be the biggest band in the world.'

Downstairs in the foyer, as the band prepared to head off to their first Stateside gig, a particularly dislikeable couple begged to differ.

'You guys are shit,' said the guy, dressed in regulation grunge gear.

'You're never going to make it in America – no British band has sold anything here in years.'

'Have you ever heard anything we've done?' asked Liam.

'No, but just look at you. I can tell. I bet you sound like the fuckin' Soup Dragons. America doesn't need you. Nothing you do matters.'

Liam started bobbing up and down, pacing in ever-decreasing circles, understandably furious.

'Listen, man,' he said, menacingly calmly, 'don't you ever tell me what I do doesn't mean anything. I can do things you can't even dream about. I'll steal your soul and you won't even notice. I've stolen it while you were standing here.'

'Bu . . . bu . . . but, Nirvana, Pearl Jam . . .' mumbled the guy tangentially, before rather queering his pitch by adopting an English accent so execrable that even Dick Van Dyke might have thought twice before taking it on board.

'Don't talk to me about Nirvana,' sneered Liam. 'He was a sad cunt who couldn't handle the fame. We're stronger than that. And you can fuck your fucking Pearl Jam too.'

The guy's girlfriend burst into tears, explaining through her sobs that Liam had just insulted the JFK of her generation. Remarkably, she was referring not to Kurt Cobain but to the dopey, hapless lead singer of Pearl Jam, Eddie 'Doh' Vedder.

'You stupid loser, corporate twats,' I chipped in helpfully at the young couple.

A full-scale scrap was only avoided by the arrival of the tour bus. And right now, in a little room somewhere in Manhattan, Lieutenant Grunge is sitting, dribbling, still railing against the hurricane.

The Nirvana 'sad cunt' quote was to dog Oasis over the next few months, although readers of the British music press rallied to defend rock's latest martyr. Noel asserted that Liam had been wrong, adding in a public statement, 'What can I say? I don't think

Kurt Cobain was a sad cunt. I think he was a genius. I think we've lost the John Lennon of our generation.'

The venue for the New York gig was called Wetlands, a small agitprop place complete with camper van at the side of the stage, Greenpeace stickers all over the place and a countryside mural painted on the wall behind the stage. Its greatest claim to fame until that point was that it hosted regular Grateful Dead nights for anyone who felt an overwhelming urge to dress in tie-dye and grow their own sandals. The air was heavy with the pervasive smell of patchouli and home-made yoghurt.

And Oasis blew the roof off.

Second on the bill, between bands called Lotion and X-CNN, Oasis were met for the first time in months by a crowd that they would have to win over. The in-house PA carried on blasting out a tape for a full two minutes after Oasis had taken the stage, despite Noel's repeated requests to 'turn the fucking music off'. It was an inauspicious beginning, but at that time Oasis seemed to thrive on taking a crowd's hostility and refashioning it into a spiky buzz, before throwing it straight back in their faces. The Wetlands gig was no exception.

And so, as someone forlornly yelped, 'Dance, you bastards, dance, you fucking bastards' throughout the set, Liam remained determinedly motionless, letting the sound of the music itself pile-drive punters against the back wall.

The short set took in 'Shakermaker', 'Fade Away', 'Digsy's Dinner', 'Live Forever', 'Bring It On Down', 'Up In The Sky', 'Cigarettes & Alcohol' (introduced playfully as 'Get It On' by Liam), 'Supersonic' and, 'the best song in the world by the best band in the world', 'I Am The Walrus'. It was stunning.

After the show, Noel concurred. 'Hey, even I thought the rest of them played well,' he admitted.

There was a bona fide New York rock celebrity in the crowd that night: Jimmy Destri from Blondie. At the time Oasis had agreed to do a version of Blondie's 'Hanging On The Telephone' for a tribute album to NY's most startling pop band. It's a project which, at the time of writing, still hasn't seen the light of day, but at the time it seemed a more than viable proposition.

So Destri turned up in the dressing-room with a bit of paper on which he'd written the chord sequences for the song. Undoubtedly aware of Noel's compulsion for appropriating any loose stitches on rock's rich tapestry and weaving them into cushion covers of his own, he'd scrawled at the bottom of the paper, 'Steal these and we'll find you.'

'Yeah, right,' said Noel, adding, once Destri had left, 'He's just scared we'll do it better.'

Liam meanwhile was half-heartedly warding off the attention of groupies, moaning to me about an incident that had taken place at the hotel the night before.

'This girl came up to my room,' he said, 'and she was fucking mad. She started dancing around, then stood on the beds with one leg on each of them and her knickers in my face. And she goes, "So, you write the music then?" and I go, "Well, no." "So you write the words?" "Not really, no." So she just gets down, walks out of the room and goes and gives him [Noel] a blow-job in the back of a cab. Bastard. I'm going to start lying from now on. "Yeah, I write everything, the words, the music, the lot."'

After the gig we'd been invited to an intriguing-sounding party by a notorious group of girls called the Rock Chicks. The invite said 'boobs and booze provided' and their apartment (later to be immortalized in the Menswear song '125 W 3rd St') had been the venue for a legendary Primal Scream party a few months earlier when Scream keyboardist Martin Duffy lacerated his stomach 'falling off the ceiling on to a load of broken beer bottles'. As you do.

Liam and I got a cab over and, as we sliced through the

streets, he confessed that the city was too overwhelming even for him.

'It's just mad,' he said. 'Everyone's running all over the place and you feel like you're in some giant film or something. I don't think anyone ever goes to sleep. I bet if you lived here, it'd do your head in.'

The Rock Chicks' Tessa Jowers (who works for a model agency) and Christine Biller (who later went on to work for Ignition, Oasis's management company) were actually far more affable and civilized than any of us had imagined and Oasis unwound in a sea of alcohol while listening to records by the Stone Roses.

Guigs sat in a corner, nursing a couple of dozen beers. 'Everyone's just going to write about them,' he said, nodding in the direction of Liam and Noel, 'and we don't mind. But it is a group and we're all involved. I think because we've known each other for so long there's always going to be that bond between us. Basically we're all here just thinking how fucking fantastic it all is. I love it.'

Tony McCarroll, sitting next to him, agreed. 'You know,' he said, 'it's going to be so depressing going back to Manchester after all this. It's like we never, ever had any doubt that all this would happen, but now it's actually happening it's still fucking brilliant. It makes you want more of it. Loads more.'

An economically opportunist by-product of the US trip was a chance for the band to shoot a video for their soon-to-be-released single 'Live Forever'. Director Carlos Grasso had decided that it would be part live performance, part vignettes (Noel: 'Vignette? Isn't that something you put on a salad.') And so, for a couple of days, the band trekked around Alphabet City participating in plenty of studiedly wacky scenarios, including Liam sitting in a chair nailed twenty feet up a wall ('I was shitting myself') and the rest of the band burying Tony alive in a sandpit with barely concealed psychopathic enthusiasm.

The 'performance' took place in a bandstand in Central Park

under the shadow of the Dakota Building. The band took advantage of the setting in order to make a pilgrimage to the John Lennon 'Imagine' memorial, and took great pleasure in imagining Yoko Ono watching the whole video shoot from her window.

Shooting schedules being what they are, the director decided not to start filming until it got dark, despite the fact that he'd gathered everyone together at noon. And so everyone kicked their heels and became increasingly pissed off with each other, distracted only by a gang of unspeakably cool rollerblader kids skating backwards down long flights of steps, setting fire to things and generally earning themselves walk-on parts as honorary members of Oasis. In fact they actually did earn themselves that role and can be seen fleetingly in the finished version of the video.

Liam, bored watching the skaters, decided to try a bit of propulsion himself. Leaping into a wheelchair that for some eternally mystifying reason just happened to be lying around, he propelled himself into the rollerblading fray and wondered aloud whether suddenly regaining the power in his legs would be the best chat-up line ever. Even the tramps kept their distance as the weirdness unfurled.

At last the director decided it was dark enough to start filming and, under the gorgeous dome of the bandstand, Oasis launched into an impromptu short set comprising instrumental versions of 'Live Forever', 'Cigarettes & Alcohol' and a new song called 'Listen Up'. Liam, buzzing at the atmosphere and frustrated at only being able to mime to repeated playbacks of 'Live Forever', decided that he'd like to do a proper show right there. So he went off to 'discuss' it with Noel, who explained the logistical impossibility of such a performance since they didn't have a PA for the vocals. Liam chose instead to interpret it as a direct snub by his brother.

'Fucking Elvis won't do it,' he grumbled as he stomped back. 'That's why I fucking hate him, the cunt. Look at this, a gig would be great. Fuck the video. Fuck the seminar. Fuck New York. Let's just do it.'

Unfortunately, it was never going to happen. Liam, still in a mood, wandered off after filming, ended up in Harlem for a bit and, perhaps due to his miraculous invincibility, somehow managed to make it back to the midtown hotel.

The next day there was still a distinct frostiness, both of the brothers accusing each other of 'acting like a pop star' and both for once treating it as an insult rather than a compliment. Much of the moodiness was compounded by the fact that they had to fly straight back to England. Despite their expressions of ambivalence about success in America, you could sense a kind of grudging satisfaction at the events of the previous days.

'It's all going to plan,' Noel told me as he waited for the car back to the airport. 'I know that we're flavour of the month or the year or whatever, but to be honest, this is exactly what we always saw was going to happen. I know exactly what we're going to be doing right up until Christmas.

'We wanted to get the album out and to release a single every three months. All those great bands like the Beatles and the Jam used to put a single out every three months, no matter where they were touring in the world. That's what we're going to do. After "Live Forever" we're putting out "Cigarettes & Alcohol" and then at Christmas a song called "Whatever". That one's going to be Top Five. No problem.'

It was to make number four in Christmas week. And a few friends who'd been equally seduced by Noel's unshakeable confidence cleaned up at the bookies.

Significantly, in the week that Oasis took America, Suede, the other current darlings of the music press, split with their guitarist and major talent in the band, Bernard Butler. Suede's foppish singer, Brett Anderson, had relentlessly bitched about Oasis in the press, at one point calling them 'the singing electricians'. Not that

Noel was unduly perturbed. 'Bernard Butler was the only talented one in the band,' he said. 'And the only person they could get to replace him is me. I've got far better things to do. I mean, I've already got our second album written in my head. I might as well start on the third.'

Oasis flew back to England, back to the increasing unreality. To a country gagging for them.

# 6

## DEFINITELY MAYBE

While the Americans would still need convincing that Oasis were more than just flashy hype, in Britain and Europe the band were building up a following that seemed to be expanding even faster than those closest to them could have hoped. It was almost happening too fast and the rest of the rest of the year would be spent trying to keep a grip on some sort of reality. It was a struggle that at times looked like a lost cause and it was here that Marcus's managerial experience was to prove more crucial than ever. Before 1994 was over, Oasis and everyone around them would experience both brand-new highs and unthinkable lows.

The first stop back in Britain was a slot at the T In The Park festival, in Strathclyde Country Park, near Glasgow, to which the journey was predictably eventful. Simon, the Cat in the Hat, takes up the story.

'Again, I'd brought the supplies and went with the band in the van up to Glasgow. Someone put the wrong sort of petrol in the van, though, and it just conked out near Carlisle or somewhere, so while we were waiting for the man from the garage everyone carried on drinking, chopping lines out on the bonnet and playing football by the side of the road. The van was out of action and there wasn't enough room for everyone to go up together, so Noel pulled me with him 'cos I had the stash and four or five of us just headed off, leaving the rest of the band to make their own way there.

'Somehow everyone made it and by the time they were supposed to go on, it was just like Glastonbury, they were all off their heads. I said to Marcus, "Can I introduce them?" and he went, "Yeah all right then." So I staggered on stage, grabbed the mic and said, "Ladies and gentlemen, the Best Rock 'n' Roll Band in the World, Oasis!!" and the crowd just went completely mad. There was this cheer I'll remember for the rest of my life and I just stood there thinking, listen to that. I'd never heard anything like it. I was gobsmacked. Then, after a bit, I was aware of this sort of shuffling behind me and I realized they were all waiting to start. They were, like, "OK, you've said your bit, now get off."

'And from the first guitar chord to the end of the set the reaction from the crowd was like they were seeing God or something. Liam was kicking footballs into the crowd and even dancing around a bit. I'd seen them at the 100 Club and then at the Marquee, where I realized what it must have been like to have seen the Who when they were starting. And that day at T In The Park you could see just how huge Oasis were going to be. They had the audience in the palm of their hand in about half a second. And afterwards everyone carried on partying until about noon the next day. It was the best buzz and around then it was happening to them almost every night.'

A couple of days later the buzz flipped into violence. Halfway through a show at Newcastle's Riverside, during 'Bring It On Down', a punter jumped on stage and punched Noel in the face. The band were immediately walking off stage and out of the venue, only to find 300 people attacking the tour bus. 'What's the point of playing to fucking monkeys?' wondered Liam out loud as they drove off, visibly shaken.

'I thought it was just some stage-diver,' says Noel. 'That's one of the songs that always got the crowds going, but it was the first time it'd actually turned into violence. So, one minute there was someone standing next to me and then, "whack", he'd got me in the face. I know when you're in a band you're supposed to just play the music, but when someone does that you react instinctively, so I just hit him with my guitar. Then we walked off and there was a riot going on outside.'

No one was sure quite why the guy had decided to hit Noel, but one rumour suggested that it was a Sunderland fan intent on an action that would most harm the chances of Oasis ever playing Newcastle again. The gig was going out live on Radio 1, so it was a particularly high-profile demonstration of regionalist lunkheadedness.

Noel was also pissed off that he'd damaged his prized guitar, the Les Paul that Johnny Marr had given him and which had played a significant part in rock history. It was the same guitar that Marr had played on the Smiths' classic album *The Queen Is Dead* and which had been a present from him to Gallagher, a symbolic passing of the torch. Before Marr, it had belonged to Pete Townshend, the very guitar that he can be seen wielding in many live pictures of the Who.

'Yeah, and some Geordie had it buried in his fucking teeth the other night,' Noel told Andrew Perry from *Select* magazine. 'I phoned Johnny up the next day,' he continued, 'and said, "I know this sounds bad, but that guitar really needs repairing." A couple of hours later a taxi pulls up outside the hotel in Leeds where we were staying and inside there was another Les Paul from Johnny. There was a note telling me what he'd played on it and it ended, "You'll like this one, it's a lot heavier and will fracture anybody's skull if you get a good swing on it."'

After Newcastle, Oasis finally appointed proper security staff around them, determined that if any destruction was going to take place, it was going to be the band themselves doing it.

A week later they made a point of proving it. Over in Sweden for the prestigious Hultsfred Festival, they found themselves sharing a hotel with Primal Scream and the Verve, two other bands who never seem to get round to packing any notion of sobriety. After the gig Oasis went back to the hotel to find a full-scale trashing session already in progress.

'I was walking into the hotel,' said Liam afterwards, 'and this chair came flying past. Then another. And another. And I thought, it's going to be a good night tonight. Everyone was just tearing the place apart and Primal Scream could see that it was getting out of hand, so they chickened out and checked out at about two in the morning. Next day we were all arrested and charged for the damage. We even got banned from Sweden and Primal Scream got off, the cunts.'

He still maintains that it was worth it.

'Oh, it was beautiful, man. I mean, I looked out of the window the next morning and the car park was, like, full of bedrooms! It took a lot of doing.'

In contrast, it was worryingly piss-easy for Liam to break a bone in his foot jumping off the tour bus a few days later.

Back in Britain, they put in their virtually obligatory performance on *Top Of The Pops*, this time to publicize 'Live Forever', their biggest hit to date, straight in at number ten.

Right from the off, it had been obvious that 'Live Forever' would be a big hit. One of the earliest songs Noel wrote for the band, it was written for his mother, but tapped in to a universal celebration of life. Structurally it echoes the big anthems from the likes of U2 and Simple Minds, but surges with an irresistible simplicity. A guaranteed arms-in-the-air classic that emphasizes

The author (centre) with Liam and Microdot designer Brian Cannon.
*Photo by Tom Sheehan*

Liam at the launch party for "(What's The Story) Morning Glory?"
*Photo by Tom Sheehan*

Oasis on their first trip to New York, for a gig at Wetlands.
*Photos by Tom Sheehan*

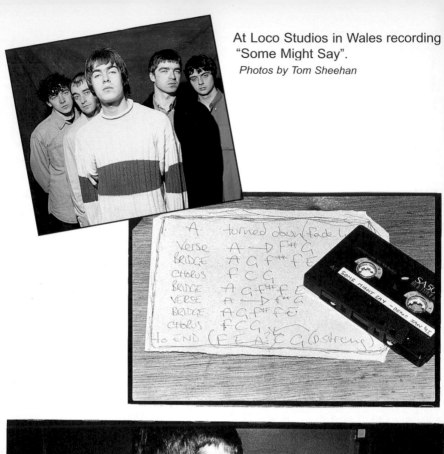

At Loco Studios in Wales recording "Some Might Say".

*Photos by Tom Sheehan*

Live in Kansas, March '95.
*Photo by Tom Sheehan*

Warming up for Glastonbury '95.
*Photo: Mark Lloyd/All Action*

Intensive training at a
charity football match.
*Photo: Justin Thomas*
*All Action*

Liam & Patsy
*Photos: Simon Meaker and Steve Volak/All Action*

'Look left, look right, wander about for a bit.'
*Photo: Mark Lloyd/All Action*

Long-time fan Tony Blair.
*Photo: Duncan Raban/All Action*

Noel's desire to write songs that defy an intellectual, considered response.

'I don't write songs that make you scratch your head and say, "What's that all about then?"' he maintains. 'I write songs that you hear once and they get straight in your head. I just keep it simple and the people who are into us understand that.'

The cover of the single, released on the twenty-fifth anniversary of the day the Beatles put out *Abbey Road*, featured John Lennon's Aunty Mimi's house in Liverpool. Parallels between the Lennon-Mimi and Noel-Peggy relationships aren't to be avoided. Live forever? Yeah, some things do.

Bracketing their *Top Of The Pops* appearance, Oasis played two impressive London shows at the Forum and the Astoria. Both of them sold out. While the sheer size of their sound had been effective in both tiny indoor venues and huge outside festivals, the two places chosen for the gigs seemed uneasily compromised, even though, in practical terms, there was no other option. On the horizon, the stadia were already beckoning.

Backstage at the Forum, the band had a special visitor. Noel's persistent championing of Paul Weller's work had brought him along to investigate and while Noel was obviously in awe of having one of his heroes in the dressing-room, he managed to keep up the cocky persona, chiding Weller for suggesting that Oasis should have done encores. 'Tell me I'm God,' he ordered Weller and for a hundredth of a second after he said it you could see him thinking, oh, fuck, was that me? But just a hundredth of a second.

'Yeah, go on, tell me I'm God.'

A few months earlier I'd met Weller at a party and drunk a couple of wine lakes to pluck up the courage to talk to him. I was pleasantly surprised to find that, while he is naturally distrustful of a music press that takes an idiotic pleasure in treating him as some sort of goonish whipping boy, he is, once he trusts you, a genuinely personable and entertaining chap. Oh, and he can party harder than most.

Weller had, back then, recently released his *Wild Wood* album, received with some enthusiasm by press and public and bringing him back into the pop fold. His career hadn't exactly been harmed by Noel's constant dropping of his name as an important influence on Oasis, but Weller himself retained an enthusiasm for up-and-coming bands, only too happy to publicly acknowledge those that he felt showed a genuine love of music. Little surprise that he and Noel bonded so quickly. And so, while the rest of Oasis would dedicate long nights to the large-scale dismantling of municipal buildings, hotels and hostelries, Paul Weller and Noel would spend their time talking about favourite records and swapping rock anecdotes. Boring to some perhaps, but to those two a constant source of mutual admiration.

'I can't do small talk,' admits Noel. 'That's why I don't like just sitting round in pubs. The only thing I can talk about for hours is music. It's just the way I am. Music is the most important thing in my life. More important than anyone or anything else.'

Two days after the gig at the Forum, Oasis played the Astoria, another fine show delivered with predictably casual ease. Afterwards they moved on to a party thrown for them at the Leisure Lounge by their old pal Simon, the Cat in the Hat. I was DJing and went along as the doors to the party opened, but no one seemed to be going in. Instead, a queue for the guest list snaked back around the block.

'They were supposed to be the last dates of the tour,' says Simon, 'so I handed out all these flyers outside the Forum and the Astoria and thought loads of the people who'd been to the gigs would come along. I spent loads on getting drinks in and stuff, but in the end there were only seventeen people who actually paid to get in. And 825 on the guest list. I lost loads on that. I think the fans just assumed that the band wouldn't turn up, like it was some big scam or something.'

In fact, Noel apart, the band stayed until the bitter end, soaking up not only all available alcohol, but also the success that made them feel lIke bulls in their very own china shop.

Despite the apparently chaotic impetus to their existence, there was a lot of careful planning, so that their immediate future was meticulously mapped out. And their work always a step ahead of itself, something which to an outsider could seem incessantly disorientating.

So, finding a few spare days after the London shows and with 'Live Forever' still in the Top Ten, they decided to make a video for their next single, 'Cigarettes & Alcohol'. The site for the shoot was the Borderline, a shoebox-sized venue off Charing Cross Road in London's West End. In the past it had been a much-used venue for secret shows and low-key performances by the likes of R.E.M. and Deborah Harry. The latter played a week-long residency there that I still remember with shivers of delight, but the Oasis video shoot was to better even that.

Word had got out about the video, as these things always seem to do among the more dedicated fans, and the telepathic telegraph ensured that a few hundred kids wearing regulation Oasis T-shirts had been waiting outside since noon. By early evening, most of them were still there, offering cash way beyond their means to anyone with a ticket. By the time it got dark, you couldn't move inside. And all this for just a video shoot.

Live performance has always provided the focus for Oasis videos and this one was no exception. Exciting in theory but rather losing its appeal when you have to watch the same song being mimed a couple of dozen times. To their credit, both band and fans managed to keep up the impression that they were part of some spontaneous new pop thrill, even after the director had given up the 'OK, just one more time' pretence and settled instead for just playing the track over and over and over again.

Before they started, and in between takes, a lone cameraman wandered around doing the hand-held thing, visibly recoiling as he stumbled into a Dionysian tableau in the dressing-room. There the wannabe groupies were out in force and the band were having fun with them, teasing out the flirtatiousness with cheeky self-assurance. By then they'd had a lot of practice. As part, no doubt, of some method-acting approach to the enterprise, they were living up to the title of the song by determinedly working their way through Bensons and booze, supplemented by the white lines of the chorus. Well, you might as well.

Some of the footage made it on to an 'uncensored' version of the video that can be seen once in a while on late-night continental TV shows that don't much care if they get taken off the air. The girl in the little pink dress who'd only just finished her O levels probably has her very own copy.

After the director finally pronounced himself satisfied with seven million miles of videotape, most of us expected the band to troop straight off to another appointment with havoc. Instead, they played some more songs, a short set including an acoustic slot by Noel. After the role recitals for the camera, you could sense the excitement they still felt at just letting rip, playing around. For half an hour they fierily reminded everyone present just why they had to make the video in the first place, the vicious, vivacious noise pinning everyone present to the spot, each chord carving THIS . . . IS . . . WHAT . . . WE . . . DO into the minds of the audience. It was breathtaking stuff.

Later the band and their entourage returned to their hotel, the Embassy, a little further west down Bayswater Road from the Columbia. 'We're working our way right along the road,' said Noel. 'We'll be in the suburbs by next week.'

At the hotel the band split, as they always did, into a number of satellite groups, from corridor to room to bar to corridor to oblivion.

The guy from the front desk came over and tapped me on the shoulder.

'Excuse me, sir.'

Uh-oh. 'Yii-es?'

'Are you with Oasis?'

'Er, yeah, sort of.'

'Have you got any skins?'

So *that* was why they let them stay so long.

A day and a half's comatose rest and relaxation and then – why the hell not? – time to tour again. Oasis were, right from the start, and indeed still are, a band whose existence revolves around playing live. Noel has the security of his songs, but for the others, particularly Liam, the real thrill, the reason to get up in the mornings, comes directly from appearing in front of an audience.

'It doesn't matter how many times you do it,' says Liam, 'it's still what matters. I'm mad for it. I always will be.'

And you don't doubt it. If he hadn't found his audience, he would have had to invent one, so important to his life is the acclaim from a crowd. He's a born performer, whether in a pub or a rock arena, and if you were to take an audience away from him you might as well just smother him with a pillow and be done with it.

In August they'd picked up a new fan, Evan Dando. Dando was singer and songwriter with the Lemonheads, a US band who'd been regularly courted by the music press, particularly in Britain, and who'd achieved moderate crossover success with their cover of Simon & Garfunkel's 'Mrs Robinson', the theme from *The Graduate*. It was a song Dando had grown to loathe, preferring people to concentrate instead on his very real talent for off-kilter songwriting: numbers like 'My Drug Buddy'. He liked Noel's songwriting and, when he'd bumped into Oasis at a festival a few weeks earlier, had enjoyed hanging out with them.

Much of the appeal came from a mutual love of partying, although Noel and Evan did write a song together called 'Purple Parallelogram', yet to be released.

Dando turned up on 30 August to accompany Oasis on tambourine at an acoustic performance in the Marble Arch branch of Virgin Megastore. It was a quirky guest appearance that gave him a cameo in a date that was to enter musical history: the day Oasis released *Definitely Maybe*. The first album, it was one that would annihilate expectations.

Despite the hours that had gone into the making of the record and the numerous studios used, *Definitely Maybe* ended up costing only £75,000, considerably less than the budget for most of the major album releases of the time. And, on first hearing, it seemed like an unsurpassable bargain.

It was everything Oasis had always promised, finally transferring the dynamic of the live performance on to record. Production work by Mark Coyle and mastering by Owen Morris, combined with Noel's insistence on 'live', had resulted in a spectacular achievement, one of the few debuts to arrive both fully formed and bursting with promise of what could come. The only previous first album to come close in its immediate impact to *Definitely Maybe* was the Sex Pistols' *Never Mind The Bollocks*. But whereas the Pistols had the same purging roar to proceedings, in addition they came emblazoned with a sense of their own self-destruction. *Definitely Maybe* was no suicide bomb – instead it was a demonstration of just how much more Semtex they had at their disposal. A big, beautiful start.

The cover even managed to convey the stillness at the heart of the tornado. The 'Supersonic' and 'Shakermaker' sleeves were deliberately neutral, the first a straightforward family portrait of the band in the studio, the second an anonymous finger poised over the play button of a tape deck in a kitschy flat. The album cover was a natural progression, the band lolling around a front room (in the Didsbury house belonging to Bonehead at the time). Around them you could make out some of their heroes, in picture frames and on TV. It was a carefully constructed reality, complete with subtly arrogant conceits like the globe hanging above Liam's head as he lay on the floor. As good an image as any of the way that the group managed to make something ostensibly natural out of a focused, calculated desire to succeed. Nothing was ever as easy as it looked.

Brian Cannon and his company Microdot, the designers of this book, have created every Oasis sleeve to date.

*Definitely Maybe* opens with a consummate Oasis song, 'Rock & Roll Star', a majestic relative of the Stone Roses' 'I Wanna Be Adored' and a number which, until recently, always constituted one of the band's rare encores. If you want to distil the hopes and dreams behind the Oasis attitude up until that moment, you don't need to listen further than the lines that declaim, 'Look at you now you're all in my hands/Tonight I'm a rock and roll star.' And as you hear it, you know that everyone else is thinking exactly the same thing. Yeah, a rock and roll star. And for three minutes you know how it feels. As with so many of Oasis's songs the 'I', 'you', 'me' and 'us' are eternally interchangeable.

The rest of the album elaborates on the opening's precision of the opening. Songs like 'Up In The Sky', 'Bring It On Down' and, particularly, 'Slide Away' are good, if not better than the singles that are also included.

The two apparently throwaway tracks, 'Digsy's Dinner' and 'Married With Children', were both born out of actual events. The first, introducing the word 'lasagne' to the rock lexicon, came from a pre-prandial remark in the studio from Noel's mate Digsy, singer with the band Smaller. 'I want lasagne!' he'd insisted. Noel made a song, if not a dance, out of it.

'Married With Children' includes the lines 'Your music's shite/It keeps me up all night', and again they were inspired by real life.

'I don't just have special times when I sit down and write,' Noel says. 'If a line comes to me, I have to write it down there and then. I was going out with this girl and one night I woke up and thought of a bit for a song, so I jumped out of bed, picked up the guitar and started trying to get it down. She woke up, turned to me, really pissed off and said, "Can't you just shut up. Your music's shite and it's keeping me up all night." I had to use it.'

On the vinyl version of the album there's an extra track called 'Sad Song', still one of the most beautiful things Noel's ever written. He never actually made a tape to send to the record company after he'd written it. Instead he debuted it live on GLR, the London radio station, dedicating it to Alan McGee.

'I was sitting listening to the radio and I heard him come on,' says McGee, 'and he played this song that was one of the best things I've ever heard. I remembered all the nights we'd hung out together in my flat and I thought, this is about me. I didn't cry – I mean, I'm a Scotsman – but it really got to me.'

Since the Monday was a Bank Holiday, the album was released on Tuesday 30 August and within days it had sold over 150,000 copies, making it not only the fastest-selling debut album of the nineties, but also arguably the biggest-selling debut of all time. It went straight to number one, beating the Three Tenors to the top spot.

In New York the previous month even people from Oasis's own record company had admitted that Pavarotti and his cohorts would probably beat them to number one the first week, although they did hold out hope that the band would eventually outsell them. Oasis themselves had little truck with such caution, resolutely believing that because their own record deserved to reach the top, it would get there. Such idealism usually ends in disappointment, but such was the momentum behind the group that all cynicism was steamrollered.

Liam was admirably calm about the album's chart-topping status and the relative merit of the Three Tenors.

'Well, of course we were going to get to number one,' he mused. 'We're loads better than three fat blokes, shouting.' So that's opera fucked then.

Not that it seemed to particularly matter to the general public, but the album also received rave reviews in the music press.

In *Melody Maker* Paul Lester wrote, 'Just buy this record before tomorrow and if you don't agree it offers a dozen opportunities to believe 1994 is the best year ever for pop/rock music, then . . . you're wrong.'

He also noted the vicarious appeal of the band: '*Definitely Maybe* is What The World's Been Waiting For, a record full of songs to live to, made by a gang of reckless Northern reprobates (yeah, we hacks love a bit of rough) who you can easily dream of joining.'

*NME* was just as fulsome in its praise. Keith Cameron, already a relatively long-term fan of the band, gave the album nine out of ten and wrote, 'here are 12 songs to hum beyond your grave'.

He went on, '30 years since the Beatles' first Number One and nearly 40 since "Heartbreak Hotel", we're somehow supposed to have evolved beyond these simple pleasures; the buzz of an electric guitar and a young voice yearning simple truths ought to leave us cold because, by definition something better must now exist. Oasis prove that this need not be so.'

The 'serious' press were just as positive. Writing in the *Independent*, Noel's broadsheet of choice, Andy Gill described Oasis as 'a classic world-beating guitar band'. He also wondered, rather optimistically, whether the title of the album might have been taken from 'the science fiction novel of the same name by the Russian Strugatsky brothers, in which the universe forcefully exerts its natural equilibrium over a world thrown out of balance'.

Unfortunately not, since Russian science fiction has never been awfully near the top of the Gallagher reading list, but it was a neat metaphor for the impact of the album.

'I'll stand by that album for ever,' says Noel. 'It is definitely one of the best first albums anyone has ever done, but it had been in my head for two years before that. By the time we'd put it out we knew exactly how it should sound.'

Despite an advertising campaign costing around £2 million, Oasis's £75,000 record outsold the Three Tenors by 20,000 copies in the first week and continued to consolidate its sales domination for months after. And it was the first number one for Creation Records.

# 7

## DEFINITELY MADNESS

After the Virgin Megastore performance, Evan Dando decided to tag along with Oasis for the duration of their short tour. His eccentric behaviour caused even Liam to describe him as 'bonkers' and he proved it the next night at a gig in North Wales. They were playing a place called the Buckley Tivoli, the only venue in the world that sounds like a pasta dish, the location chosen to give fans who didn't live in the city a chance to see the band. In fact hundreds trekked from Liverpool, Manchester and London to see them and were rewarded with a bizarre performance from Dando afterwards. As the fans left the venue, they could hear Evan singing, but didn't know where the voice was coming from. Then, as they looked up, it became clear. He was sitting on the roof, guitar in hand, serenading all and sundry like it was the sort of thing that happens all the time.

'That was nothing to do with us,' says Noel. 'Evan's just living in a world of his own. We never asked him to come along, he just sort of kept turning up.'

And he kept on turning up. Despite having been allegedly banned from Sweden only a couple of weeks later, Oasis and entourage were allowed straight back in again the night after the Buckley gig. Due to the vagaries of the international distribution network, *Definitely Maybe* had been released a week earlier in Sweden than anywhere else in the world, going straight to number one there as well and ensuring that the demand for tickets for the show had far outnumbered the capacity of the venue, Gino in Stockholm, that they were due to play. One fan allegedly threw himself off a building because he couldn't get a ticket, somewhat muting what should have been a pure celebration of success. The Swedes continue to be among Oasis's most fanatical fans.

Back to Britain, Evan still in tow, Oasis checked into a Heathrow hotel, ready for a flight to their first-ever Irish gig the next day.

'I got back to the hotel,' says Noel, 'and as I walked into the lift, out came Evan with all these police around him. Apparently he'd gone a bit wild in his room and smashed up the TV set and they'd come to arrest him. I was, like, "It's OK mate, he's with us, we'll pay for it. Now let him go." And they did.

'Next day,' he continues, 'we got to the airport and everyone was putting their bags through the metal detector. Evan put his through and suddenly all these alarms started going off. You've got to remember we were going out on a plane from Heathrow to Ireland, so it was the flight where everyone would be worried about terrorists. When the alarms went off all these guys with guns appeared from nowhere and the X-ray of Evan's bag made it look like there was a bomb in it. They were convinced he was some sort of major terrorist. Anyway, they open his bag and inside there's all these bits of metal and glass and wires. And it isn't a bomb, it's the remains of the TV he smashed up the night before. He'd felt so guilty about what he'd done that he'd just scooped up all the wreckage and put it in his bag. Like no one would notice. He's way out there, man. You've just got to stand back. Completely mad.'

That night's gig at the Tivoli in Dublin was an emotional experience for Liam and Noel, a return to their Irish roots and the first time they'd ever played there.

Oasis have, in the past, defined themselves as Irish, an impassioned if not completely convincing reclamation of their roots. At times it's seemed to have been spawned more from a desire to be awkward than anything else. But peel back the Manc scally façade and you start to comprehend the instinctively isolationist impulse that drives much of Oasis's music. Noel would never admit it, but he lives his life like he's always taking on board a first day at school, the outsider making his mark and, at the same time, confirming his otherness. Every single song that Noel Gallagher writes has traces of his Irish roots smeared between the lines. The band will always dismiss any sort of self-analysis, writing it off as a limp attempt to corral the intangible; big words trying to suffocate an uncontainable Northern soul.

The rest of the band feel free about composing their own epitaphs. Noel, one senses, prefers his to tangle inextricably in a body of work that defines not only his own personality, but also that of his mother and her mother before her. The Irish gig was the first chance to acknowledge a history that goes way past glib geographical pinpoints.

A few months earlier Noel had gone back to Ireland with his mother and his brother, Paul, and the three of them had spent a few days living in another 'real' world, a world that blithely ignored the jumped-up aspirations of would-be pop stars. There are already getting on for a dozen Oasis fanzines around, all driven by a genuine love of the band and, if they're doing it right, obsessively recording minutes of the group's existence, capturing moments that regularly elude the mainstream music press. Two of the best 'zines are *Mad For It* and *Definitely Oasis*, both of which are invaluable for lassooing those rare moments when Noel or Liam have opened up about their past.

Issue 4 of *Definitely Oasis* includes a hugely entertaining transcript of an interview that DJ Craig Cash conducted with Noel and Martin Carr from fellow Creation band the Boo Radleys on Signal

Cheshire radio in June '94. You learn not only that they're both very drunk and that Noel has decided to scrawl acute accents all over every local road sign so that Burnage can be pronounced 'Burnajay', but also that he'd recently visited his grandmother in Ireland.

'I went to see my gran,' he said. 'I hadn't seen her for years, so we went over and took some tapes and videos and the scrapbook my brother keeps of the band. We were in her cottage in County Mayo, which is really deep in Ireland and I played her an Oasis tape. She goes, "It sounds a bit like the Beatles" and I was, like, "Do you think so, Gran? Nice one." Then she says, "That's another thing, they don't seem to play the same old songs on the radio." I was going, "You'd better sit down, Gran, I've got a bit of bad news for you here. In 1970 they fell out and split up." She was really upset.'

Upset enough, apparently, to comprehend both the fact that Lennon had died after being shot five times in the back and that Elvis and JFK had quit this mortal coil, but determinedly refusing to take in the fact that Manchester United had won the double.

'She just fell over on the floor,' claimed Noel.

The jokiness barged the story away from any sense of authenticity, but in fact Noel's grandmother really was unaware of the fact that the Beatles had split up. News travels slow in County Mayo, making the Dublin gig all the more peculiar for the Eire offshoots of the Gallagher family tree.

'It was a good gig, but afterwards there was this big queue at the dressing-room door,' says Noel. 'It was all our relatives. I'd met some of them before, but there were hundreds of them who I'd never heard of. They were going, "This is your aunty's second cousin. And this is his dog. And this is someone who once saw you when you were three." They just kept on coming. I think we met half of Ireland that night.'

The next night they played to an equally ecstatic response in Belfast, before flying back home for a significant, nerve-racking experience. A gig at the Hacienda in Manchester, their first hometown gig since June.

All their answering machines were flashing like crazy when they got home as everyone they'd ever known rang up trying to blag a place on the list.

'We used to get loads of complaints from people in Manchester,' says Noel. 'They'd all be going, "Why don't you ever play here? Do you think you're too good for us or something?" Look, we spent months playing Manchester every fucking week and twenty people would turn up. If they'd been into us right from the start like they were saying, why didn't they come along to the gigs then? It's such a typical Manchester attitude.'

Old fans or not, the Hacienda was packed for the gig. At the sound check, the band had seemed relaxed, taking the piss out of one another while Noel showed off his new stash of shoes and a smart, expensive shirt. Various local luminaries mooched around, including Shaun Ryder, making one of his first appearances since the Happy Mondays had self-destructed, suited up and looking like he was only there to sell an insurance policy to somebody. Other Manchester faces kept on popping up, most of them taking time off from renegotiating record deals now that Oasis had made their pop stabs almost entirely redundant. Unsurprisingly, there was nervousness in the air, a sense that Oasis still had something to prove. Manchester, the last place in Europe to give in. Snottily stubborn to the end.

The scallies were out in force as the doors opened, touting tickets for as much as £100 a shot. An unfortunate choice of word perhaps, with the Hacienda a notorious playground for the gun gangs from Moss Side and Cheetham Hill. It was conceivable that the whole thing could turn extremely nasty and such fears looked like being realized when a few scallies managed to blag their way into the gig with perfectly copied plastic band laminates. They were stopped yards from the dressing-room door when Ian Robertson (ex-Para and newly installed last line of defence between the car thieves, dealers, gunrunners and the fuck-you rock 'n' roll band) civilly convinced them that they would be a lot better off staying well away.

It was Ian's first month in the job but, even as a Northerner myself, I couldn't come up with much of a vindication for the behaviour of the local gangs. That was one of the scariest scenarios I've ever experienced and only a couple of E's took the edge off the terror. One of the Creation entourage thought likewise and ended up so tripped-out that he came within a hair's breadth of walking up to Liam on stage and offering to buy him a drink.

The band played a brilliant, edgy set, motivated by a mixture of self-confidence and contempt, a forehead-slapping reassertion that they weren't about to stand politely beneath any kind of Manchester banner, especially if the city's lieutenants had insisted on completely missing the point of everything that Oasis represented. I'm as guilty as anybody of subscribing to the dim belief that 'people are more friendly Up North', ready to bleat blindly like some sort of latter-day Carla Lane about salt-of-the-earth sentimentalism. That night at the Hacienda persuaded me, and some of Oasis, that there'd never be any point in defending people who would grumpily piss on potential.

Oasis existed as some sort of a blueprint for an escape from the mundane, a signpost away from stupidity. Here were people trying to drag them back down, intent on destruction merely as an admission of half-heartedness. It goes against the grain of an inbuilt, dumb Northern pride, but I have to acknowledge that Oasis's success never snowballed down any sort of home-town slope. Manchester has always been just a place to stay, and to build an earnestly constructed scaffold around their geographical importance counted for nothing as soon as they got the chance to articulate a life of their own. Oasis aren't a Manchester band. They're a band from Manchester. It's much, much more than a matter of linguistics.

When you dive deep into the Manchester Business, you need

some decompression time before you head anywhere else. And when that 'anywhere else' is Japan, you really ought to take a couple of lifetimes to reacclimatize yourself. Oasis took a week, stopping off on their way to play the notoriously dull, one-horse towns of Hamburg and Amsterdam. No one slept much. And the tickets to Tokyo were non-transferable.

'I'd told the others not to be too excited about Japan,' says Noel. 'I'd been there with Inspiral Carpets and they'd gone down all right, but the audiences were really reserved and polite. I'd heard about the reputation that Japanese fans had, but after the Inspirals gigs I thought it was just people building it up. I was expecting that we'd turn up there and have a job getting people into us.'

You were wrong.

'I was wrong.'

They should have realized when they found out that the tickets for a six-date tour of the country had sold out in less than a day. Right from their arrival at Tokyo's Narita airport, through the long journey to the city itself (a good ninety minutes) and at their well-appointed, gobsmackingly expensive hotel, it started to get obvious that Noel had drastically underestimated the reactions of every girl within a 200-mile radius. Oasis might have been signed to Sony, but at the time they hadn't released a record in Japan. It didn't stop the fans mobbing them every time they even thought about going outside their hotel.

Daniela Soave, one of the few journalists who'd supported the band since the early days (at that time still only a matter of months) accompanied them to Japan for *GQ* magazine. She found their fans' reaction more hysterical than she'd ever even begun to imagine.

'I could be witnessing the second coming,' she wrote. 'Liam swaggers about insolently, carelessly shaking his crescent-shaped tambourine, or sings with his hands clasped behind his back, occasionally catching somebody's eye in the audience. Then he waves artlessly and the entire crowd melts.'

'It really was one of the weirdest weeks I've ever had in my life,' says Noel. 'There were girls coming up after every show giving us all these presents. Really expensive stuff like Beatles rarities that even I hadn't seen before. There was this one girl who followed us round to every gig, all over Japan and each night she gave me a different bit of Gaultier clothes. By the end of the tour I had a whole suit, loads of shirts, ties, everything. We had to go out and buy suitcases just so we could fill them with all the stuff they'd given us.'

For a few magical days Oasis knew what it was like to have the world revolve around them. Ringing their mates in London, they boasted that they couldn't even sound-check because of the screams from the fans drowning out the monitors.

'It made me realize what Beatlemania must have been like,' says Johnny Hopkins.

How crazy was it? Imagine the wildest scene you can think of. Then double it. A hundred times over. You would have thought that the entire population had suddenly decided that guitar songs from Burnage were some sort of essential articulation of the meaning of life. In Japan right then, Oasis were bigger than breathing.

Nevertheless, loopy Manc scally etiquette never dovetailed comfortably into any Japanese concept of hospitality, and Oasis had their best times away from the formality of corporate control. Somehow managing to swerve out of quietly insistent timetabling, they spent most nights drawn mysteriously to bars and clubs conducive to a certain Western Epicureanism. After the last of their four sell-out gigs in Tokyo, they discovered a place called the Cavern Club and, unsurprisingly, decided to pop their heads in. For five hours or so. They were even happier once they found out about the house band, a combo called the Parrots, whose set consisted entirely of Beatles cover versions.

'I'm going to live here,' was what Daniela reported Liam as saying, although he was rather less enthusiastic about the joint when only Noel was asked to contribute to a guest slot.

Later Noel explained to Soave the simple method behind his songwriting.

'The best thing John Lennon ever said,' he told her, 'was how he always went for the most obvious melody he could get, no matter how naff it sounded. And I agree. The best songs are the most obvious because the listener becomes part of the record and knows the chord change before it happens. It's like when I first heard "Hey Jude" I immediately picked up the guitar and played it. And I was only about twelve at the time.'

Ask Noel about his favourite song ever and he'll tell you it's the Beatles' 'Ticket To Ride'. He likes the way the protagonist THINKS he's going to be sad and THINKS it's today. And, most of all, like he said, he loves the way you know just before it happens that there's going to be a chord change.

He's consistently, perhaps understandably, resisted doing a cover version of 'Ticket To Ride', coming closest when doing a solo acoustic spot supporting Paul Weller and making it to the last possible moment before veering into something else. In Japan he did record a cover of 'You've Got To Hide Your Love Away', though, available on import versions of 'Some Might Say' and played for one day only on Radio 1 on International AIDS Day.

'If I cover a Beatles song,' says Noel, 'I'm just doing something that someone else has written. When we do "I Am The Walrus" we're doing a song that the Beatles never played live and I think we do it better than they would have done it. We turn it into an Oasis song. With something like "Ticket To Ride" or even "You've Got To Hide Your Love Away", it's just a copy. I don't know if I can ever write a song as good, but I'm going to keep on trying. It's the really simple songs that you hear once and think you've known all your life. They're the classics. They're the ones that matter.'

At their last gig in Tokyo, Oasis played, in their own opinion, better than they'd ever done before. And, for the first time, they did an encore.

'We did that gig in Japan and it was brilliant,' says Noel. 'None of us wanted to go off, so we decided to do an encore. It was the first one we ever did. Tony had thrown all his drumsticks into the crowd, so he had to ask for someone to give him some to play with. We did "Rock & Roll Star" 'cos that was what it was all about. That was how I felt.'

They were indestructible and even the groupies at the hotel afterwards (wandering the corridors and clambering into empty beds) couldn't take away the feeling that Oasis could do anything. That they ruled the world.

Next stop America.

'You look back,' says Johnny Hopkins, 'and you realize that, after Japan, America was going to be a complete shock to them.'

And how. Oasis flew straight from Tokyo to Seattle, still soaring on the Japanese acclaim. If they had to get a plane to get them over to America, they never noticed. They were about to crash back down to earth and the force of the impact was to almost tear them apart. The last week of September '94 was to be an unexpected and curiously necessary test of strength for the band, a few days that could have crumpled everything they'd ever worked for.

Seattle went well, the band still high on their Japanese excursion, a euphoria that was to carry them through to their next date in San Francisco and the first suggestion that the American record business was not just going to settle for the self-confident swagger that had always worked before. The day before the gig, Oasis were jumped on to the promotional conveyor belt, treated like the nobodies that, in US pan-continental terms, they still were. For the first time in ages, Noel and Liam had to plod through the whole justifying-their-existence bit.

'When you're nobody, it's the record company who tell you when the car is going to pick you up. You know you've made it when you phone and tell them when to send it. Back then we still had to do what they told us, when they wanted. We didn't like it much, but it had to be done.'

Next day they piled into the tour bus that was supposed to be their home for the next month and drove to LA. Everything was about to go very, very wrong.

In LA they'd been booked into the Hyatt on Sunset Boulevard, but after dumping their bags found themselves forced into a seemingly endless line of people asking what gave them the right to suggest that they could ever topple the grunge hierachy; how many Brits who weren't like Seal or Sting could ever hope to make an impression on the American charts; and just what was the point of a blunt, Limey take on heads-down rock 'n' roll?

And, while the interviewers treated them like shit, the record company were locked into the blankly 'hospitable' motions that you would expect from any multinational who've been brainwashed into completely dismissing any notion of passion or pure beauty. While individuals at Sony in America have always supported the band and genuinely believed in them, the workings of the Stateside record business as a whole demands that enthusiasm comes not from the heart, but from a hastily distributed memo. The superficiality that had fluttered around the edges of their previous American trip suddenly careered centre stage, making it clear that if Oasis didn't play by American rules they could kiss goodbye to US success.

Understandably, a bunker mentality took over and everyone tried to confront the situation the only way they knew. By getting completely blasted. Bonehead's brother, Martin, lived in LA and his gaff seemed as good a place as any to start a search for the self-belief that had got them so far in the first place. Dolled up, obviously, with their usual good-time abandon. Even now they won't admit they were scared, but, after Japan, it was obvious that America was going to do their heads in. And that intoxication was the most immediate way to deal with it.

They got themselves a slot on their old buddy Rodney Bingenheimer's show on K-ROQ, bizarrely overlapping with a problem phone-in and finding themselves having to offer advice to jilted lovers. Bonehead's cunning plan never wavered. 'Sue,' he said.

'Just sue. Everyone's doing it over here. Sue. Sue.' Just about everyone who rung up was urged to scurry away to a lawyer immediately.

One guy rung in asking about penis extensions.

'We've got a penis extension,' said Noel. 'He's our drummer.'

Rodney Bingenheimer rather queered his pitch by recalling the night he'd been with them when they signed, then asking about what part of Camden they were from. And a heap of expatriate Manchester callers trying to get on the guest list for the Oasis gig the next night made for jolly phone banter completely incomprehensible to anyone not living within a couple of hundred yards of Bonehead's local. Getting steadily more wasted, the band headed over to Johnny Depp's club, the Viper Room, and, almost inevitably, ended up getting thrown out. The party moved on to Bonehead's brother's and, sometime round dawn, the LAPD arrived, cautioning them about disturbing the peace. By then Noel had snatched a few hours' sleep, and the rest of the band had been up for seventy-two hours, just to see what would happen.

They found out that night at the Whiskey A Go-Go, one of LA's most famous venues and a perfect showcase for Oasis's first real imprint on America's West Coast. Even Ringo Starr turned up to check the Beatles aficionados he'd heard so much about.

He must have wished he'd stayed at home.

The gig was a complete shambles. The band were in no mood to entertain strangers and so when *NME* journalist Steve Sutherland and photographer Kevin Cummins arrived they were told to get lost. When Cummins started trying to take pictures it only exacerbated an already volatile atmosphere. Once they got on stage, things became even worse. They all had completely different set lists from each other, and consequently no one knew what songs they were supposed to be playing. When they eventually did start on one, the toll of all the partying became all the more evident. They were a mess. Liam started baiting the audience. Noel started fighting with him and, during 'I Am The Walrus', finally gave up trying to salvage anything from the night. He walked off stage.

In the dressing-room afterwards, it was time for a few home truths behind locked doors.

'I was disgusted by what had happened,' says Noel. 'It was complete shit. I said to the others, "I don't want to do this if you're not going to put everything you've got into it. If you're going to fuck around then do it when we've finished with the band. We'll have plenty of time then, but right now I'm going to be in a group who want to do something." Everyone just kind of looked around and no one said anything, so I thought, that's it, fuck it, we're splitting up.

'I took all the money from the tour float and got on the first plane out of LA. I had half an ounce of coke with me and I thought, right, I'm having this, then I'm going home. It's over.'

He went to Las Vegas and San Francisco, increasingly paranoid and convinced that the FBI were tapping his phone. Meanwhile the band's tour manager, Margaret, confiscated their passports to make sure no one else could leave. And Tim Abbot set about tracking Noel down, eventually meeting up with him and trying to convince him to get back with the others again.

'I really was ready to go back home,' says Noel, 'but in a cab to the airport I was reading a *Melody Maker* or something and, I know this is going to sound really sentimental, but I saw an advert for all these Oasis gigs in England and they were sold out. I didn't even know we were supposed to be playing half of them. Anyway, I saw the sold-out signs and I thought that if I'd been one of the people who'd bought tickets and the band had cancelled, I'd have thought Oasis were complete cunts. We'd played loads of gigs in Britain, but this was going to be the first really big tour. I knew I should go back to the others and we should sort it out.

'Honestly,' he continues, 'after that gig I really didn't want to be in Oasis any more. It had been building up for a bit and then it just came to a head. I couldn't see any good coming out of carrying on. What was happening was completely the opposite of why we'd started in the first place. We were all getting caught up in a lot of madness.'

They had a meeting and decided to give it another go, but the wounds would take a long time to really heal. Four dates were cancelled and, while 'Cigarettes & Alcohol' was released in Britain, they hung out in Texas recording some new songs. Noel rang me from Austin and admitted that things had been going badly, but laid much of the blame at the relentless meet-and-greet rituals that the record company expected them to undertake.

'I didn't come all the way here just to shake hands with some executive knobhead's wife,' he complained.

And was he friends with the rest of the band again?

'No, they're all cunts.'

I flew out for the last two dates of the American tour, in New Jersey and New York. Their brother, Paul, had also turned up (trying to blag a job at Sony as soon as the wheels touched the tarmac) along with a sizeable Mancunian contingent.

During the first half of the New Jersey show, it was obvious that there was still a lot of animosity between band members, none of them even looking at one another, let alone speaking. And something was missing from the sound. It had no heart. Halfway through the set, perhaps inspired by the Brit presence, they started to turn things around, tentatively restored some of the old magic. By the time they played New York the next night, again at Wetlands, they'd got the old spirit back. That they did an encore, suggested that the wheels were back on the wagon.

After the gig the Rock Chicks again hosted a party for the band and Noel played a song he'd written while on the run. 'Talk Tonight' was the finest thing he'd ever written, a melancholy reflection on his state of mind as he headed for Vegas, full of allusions to a girl he'd met in San Francisco who'd provided some sort of redemptive presence.

'I may have been completely pissed off,' he said, 'but it wasn't going to stop me writing songs. Nothing ever will.'

# 8

## BEST NEW BAND

Having somehow managed not only to salvage something from the American madness, but also to rediscover something of a sense of purpose, Oasis came back to Britain to find 'Cigarettes & Alcohol' at number seven in the charts, their biggest hit so far. While the sleeve of the single (featuring band and friends including, centre stage, Tim Abbot, at a party-cum-photo shoot in a room at London's Halcyon Hotel) might have suggested intentions of a life of hedonistic leisure, the closing months of the year were spent touring extensively in Britain and Europe, consolidating both their renewed vigour and their ever-growing popularity. *Definitely Maybe* topped charts right across the continent, as well as notching up healthy sales as far away as Australia. They were fast shaking off any appearance of just another indie band, crossing over at last into mainstream success.

At a *Q* magazine awards ceremony in November, held in a plush Piccadilly hotel, Noel, on the way back from a restorative trip to a toilet cubicle, found himself face to face with Tony Blair. Buzzing off his head, Gallagher could just about manage a few words of good luck to the Leader of the Opposition, but was shocked to discover that Blair owned a copy of *Definitely Maybe* and played it in the car every morning on the way to work. You don't get much more mainstream than that.

They even managed to duck the censors with the lyric on 'Cigarettes & Alcohol' and how 'you might as well do the white line'.

'You have to give radio stations the lyrics,' says Noel, 'so we just said Liam was singing "you might as well do the white LIME". We made up some story about how the whole song was about eating fruit. And they believed us.'

By the end of the year, Oasis would have played 120 gigs in twelve months and the burst of activity in November and December was never likely to be entirely trouble-free. At a gig at Glasgow's Barrowlands Liam's voice finally gave out and he stormed off stage, leaving Noel to take over for the rest of the set. The audience started to get angry, even more so when their security guy forgot that the mic was on as he walked on stage and told Noel that the bus was out the back with the engine running, ready for a quick exit. A riot was just about avoided, but not before promises were given to reschedule the gig. It did, however, re-emphasize Noel's growing vocal confidence. Like everyone else, he understood that no one could ever dominate a stage quite like Liam, but it made him increasingly confident of handling vocal duties on more of the songs.

In December Oasis released their fifth single in nine months and only just missed out on a Christmas number one.

'Whatever' was the song that Noel had written almost two years earlier and promised would be Top Five at Christmas '94. That he was right was almost taken for granted, such was the confidence in the Oasis camp. It made number three, beaten only by East 17 and Mariah Carey, and even then the difference in sales was just a matter of a few thousand. Importantly, it brought in a whole new audience with its undisguised homage to the Beatles and lush string section. Early demos of the song included a couple of lines from 'All The Young Dudes', but threats of legal action from David Bowie meant that they had to change them for the final release. Still, an older audience who hadn't been able to handle the speedball buzz of the earlier singles found it much easier to appreciate the classically melodic structure of 'Whatever', which sold over 200,000 copies and still shifts at a healthy rate almost two years later. As does the debut album. It had gone platinum by the end of '94 and hasn't been out of the higher reaches of the Independent Album Chart since its release.

The band ended the year with two big gigs in Brighton and Middlesbrough. At the former, Liam found himself a new, if annoying admirer. Paula Yates latched on to him at a party after the gig and wouldn't let him out of her sight, causing him to conclude 'that woman is completely mad. I keep on telling her to fuck off, but she won't listen.' The next day, on the wall behind her bed on the set of *The Big Breakfast*, Paula had stuck up a photo of Liam. Perhaps he hadn't made his point clearly enough.

In fact it was another admirer that was to prove rather more enduring. At a gig in Cambridge a month earlier Chrissie Hynde from the Pretenders had brought her friend along to see the band and meet Liam afterwards. He and Patsy Kensit hit it off right from the start.

I recall a late-night conversation with Liam in a hotel bar sometime earlier. I asked him whether he'd ever been in love.

'No,' he replied. 'Only this close.' And he spread his arms as far apart as he could to elaborate.

'The thing about love,' he said, 'is that some people think it's like the Derby, when in fact it's like the Grand National.' A typically Confucian response from Liam, but not without its profundity. He knew that if he was going to make any relationship work he would have to learn to deal with a whole load of obstacles. And he wasn't going to fall in love until he knew he'd be able to deal with them. If 1994 had been hectic, the New Year didn't look like being any different. Marcus and the band were convinced of the importance of maintaining the momentum that had built up, particularly in America. 'I told them that getting their success was like steering a boat,' says Marcus. 'In England and, to an extent in Europe, it's just like being in a little dinghy. You can turn around or move in a different direction really quickly. In America it's like you're steering an oil tanker. If you want to turn you have to think about it and plan for it a long way ahead. Everything takes a lot longer. I saw Led Zeppelin as a good model for Oasis and the way that they could make it in America. They didn't need to use the media. Instead they'd built up an audience directly, but establishing themselves as a live act. That's what Oasis could do. And, they've done it.'

So the band spent the first four months of the year building up their transatlantic Air Miles and finally beginning to see their persistence paying off. One gig in Atlanta elicited a particularly enthusiastic response and it left an enduring image in Liam's head.

'They were mad for it,' he'd told me on their return. 'All the fans were hanging from the ceiling like bats.'

There'd also been the usual share of high jinks. Liam had gone out on the town with Dave Gahan the night after the Depeche Mode singer had tried to commit suicide and ended up on a bizarre cab ride with a driver who'd never heard of Oasis and who kept on telling Gahan that he was supposed to be dead. Depeche Mode had actually established themselves as one of the most popular 'alternative' acts in America, regularly filling stadia, particularly on the West Coast. Before long, Oasis would eclipse even Depeche's success and in early '95 the first signs were evident that the hard work was paying off. *Definitely Maybe* had sold almost 250,000 copies in America and had made the Top 75 of the album charts. It may not sound like much, but it marked a real breakthrough, not just for Oasis themselves, but for British bands generally. And, as 'Live Forever' went to the top of the US college charts, trade bible *Billboard* ran a front-cover story confirming the British invasion of the radio charts. They weren't yet competing with the big boys, but for the first time in years the Americans were starting to take British rock 'n' roll seriously.

Noel, however, was becoming increasingly annoyed with the meet-and-greet rigmarole.

'I just tried to avoid them whenever I could,' he says. 'One day they threw this meal for us and I told them beforehand that I'd only turn up if there were certain conditions. So we're sitting at a table and before we start, this guy from the record company gets up and says, "Noel Gallagher has told me that he is only here to have his dinner and no one is to say a single word to him at any time." So I had my food, then got up and as I walked out, everyone clapped. Dickheads.'

Nevertheless, the band managed to make it through their American dates without too many signs of combusting, although Noel did manage to crack his head open in a go-karting accident in Virginia, and one of the band got off with a girl who started beating him up during sex, making the rest of them think he was getting murdered. Those blips apart, it all went surprisingly smoothly. At a New York show where they thought they'd played badly, they even got solace from another superstar fan, John McEnroe.

'We met him afterwards and he was great, a complete mad bastard,' recalls Liam. 'He had a spliff and a drink and told us he really liked us and that he was in a band himself. He started singing this song all about "You cannot be serious/Double faults hurt my head" and I'm going, "Yeah, nice one." He's fucking mad.'

*Guardian* writer Jim Shelley hooked up with the band halfway through the tour and found Noel in voluble mood. Gallagher even explained that he had medical reasons for his cocaine use. The last time he'd been in Detroit he'd stayed up for days, convinced that if you went long enough without sleep eventually you'd be able to stay up for ever, a somewhat bold new interpretation of received medical opinion and one that not too surprisingly ended with him being rushed to hospital.

'The doctor came up to me,' Noel told Shelley, 'and he went, "It's a good job you're twenty-seven, 'cos if you were forty-seven you'd be dead." Before I went away, though, I went to my doctor in Harley Street and he told me I had really low blood pressure. That's why smoking a draw was my only problem. Every time I had a spliff I'd faint. The doctor said, "Basically you're all right with anything that gets you going, 'cos you need that." I love my doctor, man!'

Noel also revealed that the band didn't actually have a management contract with Marcus – rather that it had all been sealed simply on a handshake. And if Marcus ever tried to sue him?

'I'd burn his house down, and he knows it.'

Back home, the awards were starting to roll in. At the Brits they picked up Best New Band, although they felt that they ought to have won more. Their frustration was compounded by the fact that Blur swept the board, although to their credit, the latter did suggest in their acceptance speech that their Best Band award should have been shared with Oasis. Oasis should have taken the olive branch and responded with some sort of grace, but such was their single-mindedness at the time that they saw no space for compromise or conciliation. You were the best or you were nothing.

Oasis were more successful at the *NME*-sponsored Brats awards, picking up 'Best Band', 'Best New Band' and 'Best Single' (for 'Live Forever'). Noel's acceptance speech acknowledged the importance of the support of the fans, but he also made sure he got a few indiscriminate insults in towards most of his peers, claiming that every other band present was 'crap'.

At the party afterwards at the Raw Club under the YMCA he

was a lot friendlier, but later blamed his bonhomie on the effects of the Ecstasy that he'd been knocking back all evening. Somewhere along the line he even managed to lose one of the statuettes he'd been presented with earlier.

Afterwards a few of us went back to Noel's place. In fact Johnny Marr had let him use his home in Fulham, a gorgeous flat that impressed on Noel the kind of luxury that accompanies real success. It was in the same block, complete with inch-thick glass in the windows, as Salman Rushdie's safe house. The situation wasn't entirely conducive to the narcotically fuelled paranoia in those present and everyone insisted on sitting well away from the front of the building.

Noel was raving about a new song he'd written, and played a rough demo tape. A stirring pop song, one of the most self-contained, complete things he'd yet come up with, it had been the product of feverish songwriting during the few days he'd had off at the turn of the year, a time when he'd written much of the stuff that was to turn up on their next album.

Before he played the tape of the new song, I jokingly asked him what he'd ripped off this time.

He didn't even pause.

'"Ooh La La", by the Faces. It's a top tune.'

The song was 'Some Might Say' and it was finally to give Oasis their first number one.

# 9

## HE'S MY BROTHER

We were lost. Completely. Photographer Tom Sheehan and I had been invited to Loco Studios in South Wales, where Oasis were to record their single 'Some Might Say'. Unfortunately, we'd trusted our safe passage to a cab driver with apparently even less local knowledge than we had.

Things seemed to be going well as we cruised through the outskirts of Newport, a place decorated with town-symbol cherubs that graced the sleeve of the Stone Roses' single 'Love Spreads' (and consequently got stolen by overeager fans every half-hour). As soon as we hit the first sign of countryside, however, the cabby decided to take us on a scenic tour of muddy dirt tracks lined with rotting foxes and that corrugated-iron-and-bits-of-rope detritus that farmers delight in passing off as a viable alternative to proper buildings.

'This cabby, he's not exactly Vasco da Gama, is he?' noted Sheehan as we drove past the same rusty ploughshare for the hundredth time.

After a mere four or five hours we finally located Loco Studios, hidden behind a hedge and signposted merely by a small pile of white stones. Still, easier to remember than the names of any of the local villages, all of which seemed to be paying tribute to a particularly nasty, vowel-free hand of Scrabble.

The studio itself is a kind of technological Tardis, contained in what looks like a converted folly, complete with accommodation, a tree house and the sort of views guaranteed to unblock even the most bunged-up of creative impulses.

'I love the countryside. I'm mad for it,' announced Liam as soon as we arrived. Hardly what you'd expect of a child of the city, a twenty-four-hour-party person with a notoriously low boredom threshold. After all, the studio engineer had already noted the fact that the journey for a packet of Rizlas involved a thirty-five-mile round trip.

'Nah,' said Liam. 'I love it.'

But what would he find to do? I wondered.

'I'd get a full-length mirror, stand in front of it and have a ruck with myself. Cities do my head in.'

He still had three days recording to go.

Much of the instrumental work had already been done and Bone-head, Guigs and Tony were ready to head back to Manchester. Liam would stay to record his vocals, just as soon as Noel had finished writing them, then Noel and producer Owen Morris would tinker with things until they'd found the 'perfect' Oasis sound. There would be arguments. Obviously.

For a moment at least, though, they were buzzing at the very real prospect of achieving the full-blown success they'd promised for so long, a show of strength that would lift them above the level of mere indie chancers. A vindication of their glorious arrogance. This atmosphere of solidity was enhanced by the presence of Bonehead's eight-week-old daughter, Lucy Oasis. It's safe to say that while she may be the first person ever blessed with that name, she is unlikely to be the last.

'Noel's the godfather,' revealed Bonehead's fiancée, Kate, prompting the thought that the poor child was destined to receive birthday gifts of guitars and Beatles bootlegs for the rest of her days.

'No,' said Kate. 'He's really good. He got her lots of fluffy toys and things.'

Not that Noel had entirely forsaken his musical enthusiasms. He showed me the plectrum he was going to use to play the guitar lines on 'Some Might Say', an ultra-rare Beatles souvenir with 'George Harrison' etched on it.

'Top, eh?' he said. 'It's going to be the inspiration.'

The early tape of the session was noticeably different from the demo that he'd played a week earlier. Far harder and less noticeably indebted to the Faces, it was, even at such a ragged stage, undoubtedly a classic in the making.

'Just wait until it's finished,' he promised. 'Number one. No problem.'

He also revealed that he'd solved the problem of what other songs were to go on the single, playing me first a track called 'Acquiesce'. The title has already been used by the highly literate Elvis Costello acolyte Aimee Mann, but it's not the sort of word you'd expect the determinedly direct Noel Gallagher to use.

'I was watching the O J Simpson trial on TV and it came up in that,' he revealed. 'I didn't have a clue what it meant, but it sounded a dead good word. I looked it up and it said it meant being dragged into something no matter how hard you try and resist. Like the Pied Piper or something. It seemed pretty apt for Oasis. People hear us and they acquiesce. Heh heh heh.'

How long did it take to write?

'Twenty minutes, max. I was on the way down to the studio and the train broke down, so I thought I might as well do something to use up the time. I always write best when I'm under pressure or pissed. It's better just doing it in a burst than spending months going back and fiddling with everything. Most of the best things we've recorded have been done really quickly. I mean, we take a weekend to do four tracks for a single and they turn out brilliant. Some bands would lock themselves up for six months and mess around with everything so much that all the passion just disappears from it.'

'Acquiesce' remains one of the most extraordinary songs Noel has ever written. Not just because of its inherent rock 'n' roll quality (Noel: 'Everything we do is a classic, other bands could make careers out of the stuff we use for B-sides') but because it's one of the few Oasis songs to address, albeit ambiguously, the relationship between the Gallagher brothers. The 'We need each other. We believe in each other' chorus could easily be a straightforward boyfriend/girlfriend litany, but it's tempting to see it as the closest the Gallaghers have ever got to a sort of fraternal 'I've Got You Babe'.

'It's like I've said, I'm not always comfortable writing personal songs,' Noel revealed. 'It's never been what we're about. I mean, I read Eddie Vedder from Pearl Jam talking about being abused as a child and how he draws on that in his songs and I just think, fuck off, don't tell ME about it. I don't want to know. When I wrote "Talk Tonight" and "Slide Away" I realized I could write personal songs, but they're always in the minority of what we do.

'Our strength comes from the fact that we write really good, straightforward pop songs. Or rock songs. I've got one called "All Around The World" that was written years ago and I've always said it could win the Eurovision Song Contest. Maybe one year we'll enter. With that song, we'd fucking walk it.'

As Noel waited to play the new mixes to Liam, he mused on the state of their publicly stormy relationship.

'Hey, man, I love him, he's my brother. We don't fight any more than any other brothers, it's just that we don't bottle things up. If we get pissed off with each other about something, we just get it out in the open, punch each other and get over it. I mean, I get pissed off if his voice fucks up, but I know it's only because we've been working so hard and his voice needs a rest. You can't keep it up for, like, two years solid.'

I wonder whether Noel really understands Liam, knows what makes him tick.

He told me in Wales that the two of them were very different in their most basic of impulses.

'I haven't a clue what he's really thinking. It's like he's at war with the world, but I don't know why. There's something really getting to him, but I don't know what it is. He's always questioning everything, looking for answers. With me it's like life's just a load of questions. If I don't find the answers, then fuck it, they'll turn up later on. Our kid doesn't want that, he just wants to know all the answers right now, this minute.'

Before recording his vocals for 'Some Might Say', Liam went off into Newport for an afternoon's drinking and shopping session. He returned after an extensive pub crawl with a couple of jumpers, a copy of Nirvana's *Unplugged* album and writer's cramp from having signed about a million autographs. All this surprisingly without getting into anything approaching a fight.

'He always gets recognized,' moaned Noel. 'I never do. Or if I do then it's always some kid who comes up to me and says, "Hey, are you Noel from Oasis?" and if I go, "Yeah, I am," they go, "No, you're not." I don't know why they bother really. They always seem to think I'm just someone who looks a bit like me. I should get a T-shirt that says "Yes It Is. Really". All this celebrity thing is just fucking weird.'

Liam was well tanked up by this point and began bobbing around the studio kitchen, answering some more of those questions that ricocheted inside his head. And demonstrating that mixture of spirituality, passion and scatter-gun stream of consciousness that makes him so endearing to anyone who ever spends any amount of time with him.

'Do you think we go anywhere after we die?' he asked himself as much as anyone else, demanding that everyone within earshot witness him running through the options.

'I live for now, not for what happens when I die,' he shouted, cigarette in one hand, Jack Daniel's in the other, pacing up and down with that familiar pimp-roll walk.

'If I die and there's something afterwards, I'm going to hell, not heaven. I mean, the devil's got all the good gear. What's God got? The Inspiral Carpets and nuns. Fuck that.'

As evangelical agnosticism goes, you'd be hard pushed to find a more convincing argument.

I wondered what his epitaph would be?

He didn't even blink.

'When I die,' he said, 'I want them to write on my grave, "Don't Fucking Come Here With Your Bunches Of Flowers". I don't even want a gravestone, I want a V-sign, two fingers. A really fucking huge V-sign, twenty-foot tall or something. When you're dead, you're dead. It's now that matters.'

At war with the world, even in the afterlife.

Making a single isn't something you find in a textbook and Oasis, more than anyone, refuse to follow rules. Over the three days I spent with them in Wales they seemed to do most of the recording in impulsive bursts. Just when you thought they'd nipped out for a piss or something, they'd come back with yet another song recorded. Just sort of exploding behind your back.

They did take time off to watch *The Word* on TV. A clip of their first performance on the programme won the viewers' vote for the footage they most wanted to see again, attracting twenty-eight per cent of the registered votes. Oasis walked it.

'That meant a lot to me,' Noel admitted the next day. 'Twenty-eight per cent is pretty good. I've never done what I do for anyone else, but, you know, those people who rung in. It proved we're right.'

'You're wrong. That's shit.' That's Liam. Sitting at the mixing desk, he'd just heard the putative first mix of 'Some Might Say'.

'It's not shit, it's great,' replied Noel.

'No it's not, it's shit. It's weird.'

'It's meant to be weird.'

'Yeah,' says Liam, 'weird to everyone else, not to us.'

'What do YOU think?' Liam asked, turning to me and putting me in perhaps the least enviable position in the whole world, in the middle of an argument between the Gallaghers.

I thought about pretending to be either mute, French or dead. For a moment I even entertained the still more ludicrous concept of trying to engender some sort of compromise, a hopeless belief in the healing power of the middle ground. In the end I just coughed for ages until they both got bored and went outside to push each other round for a bit.

Finally Noel returned to twiddle more knobs with producer Owen Morris, the only person outside the band who instinctively understands 'the Oasis sound'. Liam and I went off for a drink.

'See what happened then?' he said. 'That's what happens all the time. That's why people say we're always fighting. I'm just standing up for myself. He thinks it's his band and we're all supposed to be sheep. The rest of them go along with it, but I'm not going to. I mean, if he told them all to turn up tomorrow because we were going to play a gig under a lamp post, they'd just do it. I'd ask him, "Why are we playing up a lamp post. Can't we play a stadium or something?"

'It's like when Bonehead's girlfriend was pregnant,' he continued. 'If I'd found out my girlfriend was pregnant I wouldn't have gone on the tour. I'd have just said, "Fuck it, there's more important things."'

And, while he wasn't denying the importance of Noel in shaping the band's sound, he wasn't about to give his brother sole credit.

'We're not just old Bartholomew's backing band like he some-times thinks. I mean, he wouldn't have joined if I hadn't been there in the first place. If he hadn't joined we might have been shit or we might have ended up being good. I wrote three songs back then and I admit two of them were shit. The other one was all right, though. And I wrote the chorus to "Columbia". I'm not useless. And I'm going to start proving it. I've given up the pot and I'm cutting back on the boozing. You waste so much time when you're just pissed and lazy. I'm going to learn to play the guitar properly and write some songs.'

Would Noel welcome the creative input from him?

'No, of course he fucking wouldn't. I remember I said to him, "If I came up to you and I'd written something as good as 'Hey Jude' – I know it's not likely, but if I had – would you let us record it?" And he went, "No, I'd quit." It really hurt when he said that. I mean he writes all these words for me to sing, like "Noel's gonna tell you what you're gonna do" and "I wish I wasn't me" and I still sing them. I don't complain about that to him because I know he writes brilliant songs, but I don't think he should just ignore my ideas.

'It's like when we were on the last tour. I had an idea for backing vocals on one of the songs, but when I told him, he just went, "No, that's shit." Then when we did the song, he started doing backing vocals just like I'd said. I went, "I told you that would be good," but he went, "No, they were different backing vocals." He's just too proud to admit that I'm right sometimes.

'There's only a few songwriters that really inspire me. People like John Lennon and Paul Weller. And Noel's up there with them. I'm not going to pretend that he isn't. I just wish he'd remember sometimes that Oasis is a band.'

And, for ten minutes at least, I suddenly found myself in that band too. As the alcohol and pharmaceuticals helped to dissipate tensions, Noel suggested that we all help out with handclaps. So a motley crew, including me, the band's press officer Johnny

Hopkins, Oasis sleeve photographer Michael Spencer Jones and a girlfriend of Liam's called Kadamba, trooped into the studio to clap along to no more than ten seconds of music which would then be looped throughout the song. A seemingly simple task, but one which found us plumping for a passable impersonation of a group of disorientated performing seals. A couple of hours later producer Owen Morris finally pronounced himself satisfied. Presumably to avoid further damage to his forehead from banging it on the mixing desk in frustration.

Back upstairs, Noel and Liam were embarking on a kind of scrap-by-proxy as they watched the Benn-McLellan boxing match. Noel was supporting Benn, so, with a reassuring inevitability, Liam decided that McLellan was the greatest fighter in the history of the game, valiantly insisting that McLellan had thrown the contest even as the defeated boxer was taken away to hospital in a coma.

Before they had time to recreate the fight in the corner, Morris returned to play the final mix of 'Some Might Say'. Four minutes later most of us were conclusively convinced that it would provide the band with their first number one. The original demo had been beefed up, layered with a glorious, affirming noise, but still shot through with an irresistible melodic brilliance. Yeah, number one. The only person who didn't seem surprised poured himself another drink.

'Yeah, of course it'll be number one,' said Noel. 'That's what it's there for.'

# 10

## HAVE MORE PARTIES

A week's a week in the real world. Round Oasis, seven days can stretch into an eternity. Or twang into a kind of reassuringly self-contained microcosm of their entire existence. And, no matter how long you know them, how many times you see them hurtle in one end of the tunnel and out seven days later, you're never quite prepared for the events that might have taken place in between. Most of the time, neither are they, although they'll deny it, like those 'careful' drivers who never get into accidents but just seem to see a lot happening all around them. And if there was ever a week for audacious joyriding, it was 17–22 April 1995.

There was a plan. A loose-limbed adventure taking in three gigs in Southend, Paris and Sheffield, complete with tour T-shirt. A pan-European challenge that was met by more fans than even the group themselves could have imagined, a vociferous show of faith that was not without its inevitable casualties. Those of us who were there look back on it, like the band, with both a sort of crazed fondness and a wistful acknowledgement of innocence necessarily abandoned. For the only time in their career, Oasis were in a hurry, impatient to take their own existence away from extended promise and into truly obliterative stardom. It was the week they decided to Make It Big.

Monday 17 April 1995. The band's first full-length UK show of the year. Sold out since the dog-end of winter and ticket touts charging upwards of £50 a pop. The name 'Oasis', marked out in lights across the front of Southend Cliffs Pavilion, shone across the bay with a neat classicism far removed from the gaudy fairground 'n' fish bar vulgarity a few hundred yards down the coast. It defined a dizzying future rather than tarted up an increasingly unreal past.

But maybe there was, after all, an empathy with the run-down seaside environment. The venue was certainly more used to accommodating modern-day vaudevillian entertainment than heads-down rock 'n' roll – as the bright green posters for forth-coming shows by Jimmy Tarbuck and Kenny Lynch testified – and the seventy-year-old ushers seemed ill prepared for an invasion of surly teenagers, many of whom were so drunk by the time the doors opened that they merely flopped inside the foyer and slept off their hangovers for the rest of the evening. Those not comatose by the time support band the Verve came on, spent much of the rest of the evening in dedicated pursuit of such a state, drinking the bar dry with little difficulty.

It was a marvellous, grubbily Bacchanalian atmosphere, but somehow blurred the focus of the performance by Oasis them-selves. Sure, there was power and passion, thunder under the lighting. But there was also a messiness to the proceedings, a sense of some cult religion not yet fully focused, torn this way and that by mere bluster. If later gigs were to be rock 'n' roll war, this, particularly in retrospect, was more like a fight at a wedding reception.

It didn't help that the gig was being filmed (it was later to be released as a long-form video under the title *Live By The Sea*), an operation that required at least an element of control, of manipulation. The audience, many of whom, memory insists, were actually eating chips, filled the gaps between songs with football chants and drunken psychobabble, no bad thing in itself, but not best appreciated by an already obstreperous Oasis.

The internal cracks in the band that were to come to a head a few days later ensured that they spent much of the set sniping among themselves. When someone in the crowd threw a trainer at Liam it seemed as though they might sack the whole night and just walk off the stage. But then, as they've done so often, they somehow turned it around.

'I was too pissed to remember much of that gig even when it was happening,' says Liam. 'I know there'd been lots of arguments and I got, like, "Fuck you," when that shoe got thrown. I looked over at our kid and he was just, like, in a world of his own. So I thought, well we're the best band in the world, we might as well prove it.'

The last twenty minutes pulled things together, the band almost casually appropriating a new-found vigour. By the time they concluded with the by now obligatory 'I Am The Walrus', they had even redirected the crowd's energies into wide-eyed approval. Or maybe it was just the drink.

In the dressing-room afterwards, the white lines racked out and the alcohol flowing like Niagara, the band seemed pleased to have got the year's first British show out of the way, happier yet that their fan base appeared now to have risen into the thousands. There was an impromptu party in the venue afterwards, the organization of which was conducted entirely by old men with walking frames who had to be continually reminded what century it was, let alone where they were or where the party might be. Fearing they might drive already deeply bewildered old people into insanity, the band left, ready for the next leg of the jaunt. As they set off, Liam was arguing with Tony, the drummer. It was an argument that would never end.

Thursday 20 April. Paris. Although you wouldn't have known it by the coachloads of scallies from Liverpool, Manchester and London who barged through the doors of the Bataclan club, swaggering in the joyful, cocky discovery that they'd finally found a band who came on as just a bigger, better version of themselves. In reality, few if any of the crowd could ever carry off the business of scruffy stardom with anything approaching success; certainly none of them could come close to making such glorious music. But at least Oasis had the same roots, and behaved the way the fans liked to think they would too. With Oasis, they could dream.

Not that the British contingent made up the whole audience. By then, Oasis had already built up healthy sales in France of *Definitely Maybe* (the record company presented them with silver discs in the dressing-room beforehand) and 'Whatever', only just released over there, was already in the Top Five. Hence a voluble, enthusiastic young Parisian presence with just about everyone joining in with every word. Remarkably, although its British official release was still three weeks away, an awful lot of people seemed to know all the words to 'Some Might Say'.

It was one of the greatest gigs Oasis have ever played, perhaps because they all knew it was a final goodbye to small venues, a farewell to having to be defined by anyone else's ideas of what was possible. From here on in, they were going to start writing their own rule book.

And the first rule read: 'Have More Parties'. So in a small Left Bank club that was better suited to beatnik boho conversations Oasis proceeded to prove once again that you can take the lads out of Manchester, but even a continental jazzbo ambience stands little chance of taking Manchester out of the lads.

In the absence of any Class A stimulants, a little improvisation was required. Noticing that I'd brought over a packet of ProPlus, Noel decided to experiment with the recommended dose.

'Hey, Paul. Do you think sixteen will do the trick?' he shouted across the bar.

'Oh, I expect so,' I replied.

'Well,' he decided, 'save me some more for later just in case it doesn't.'

Somewhere between an hour and a minute later, someone decided that we'd better leave.

Next, it was on to a rather classier potential wreckage, a chrome-railed bar where champagne cost £150 a bottle. Oasis proceeded to get through nearly £3000 worth before Liam vaulted straight to the source, apparently under the impression that if we drank enough there would come some point where you were legally entitled to just, like, help yourself.

'It only seemed fair,' he said, as we left, rather too rapidly to appear entirely insouciant. Noel was grinding his teeth as we somehow made it back to the hotel.

In the hotel bar a 'quick' drink appeared to have all the makings of total madness until a fight broke out between Liam and Tony. The argument that had been simmering, certainly for days, more probably for months, was concluded when the singer of the greatest rock 'n' roll band in the world punched out the drummer.

Noel has always been somewhat more selective in his pursuit of oblivion, ever since the early days tending to go off alone rather than roar incomprehensibly at his compadres over gallons of alcohol. That night was no exception and, cranked up on industrial quantities of ProPlus, he headed off to his room.

'I've got a song to finish,' he told me. 'I was listening to this John Lennon bootleg and it's got this great line about "the brains I had went to my head". I'm having that.'

'What, you're just going to nick it?'

'Well, yeah. I mean, it'd be a shame to waste it. The song's going to be a classic.'

I woke up the following morning in a luxurious but empty hotel room in a completely different *arrondissement*, holding a big brass key. A key that didn't belong to either the room I was staying in or the one I'd originally checked into in a hotel across town. To this day, I have no idea who it belonged to or how it got there.

On the newly opened Eurostar train back to England for the third leg of the tour, we found out that one of the Verve, the band who were due to support Oasis in Sheffield, had got his arm broken in an altercation with, well, someone, somewhere. And Liam and Tony were never going to talk to each other again.

It wasn't even the weekend yet.

Saturday 22 April. Sheffield Arena is one of those huge, purpose-built venues that lie on the outskirts of nearly every major British city, equally at home with an ice-hockey match or a fruiterers' convention as a rock gig. Such was the demand for tickets that the whole area had been cordoned off and touts had to relocate to the ticket barrier at the main railway station. With over 10,000 people, it was Oasis's biggest gig to date. And a hint of just how big they were about to become.

Inside the venue Oasismania had reached fever pitch. Ocean Colour Scene, another of the bands who owe their resurgence to the Gallagher seal of approval, kicked off the proceedings, followed by Pulp, last-minute stand-ins for the injured Verve.

'The day before the show I had no idea what I was going to do that weekend,' Pulp's Jarvis Cocker recalls. 'It was ridiculously short notice, but I'm glad we did it. If we'd had more time to think about it, we'd have been really nervous about playing a home-town gig, but we just went ahead and did it and it was one of the best gigs we've ever done.'

Pulp closed their set with one of the first live performances of 'Common People', the song that was to turn them from long-time strugglers into mainstream stars and a number that seemed to carry particular resonance for Oasis's determinedly 'common' fan base.

By the time Oasis came on, the atmosphere was white-hot and any doubts about whether they could carry off the stadium-rock

The Loch Lomond and Knebworth shows. Big stuff.
*Photos: Suzan Moore and Justin Thomas/All Action*

Noel guesting at hero Burt Bacharach's Royal Festival Hall Show.
*Photo: Simon Meaker/All Action*

Under seige. Liam with
Patsy's son, James.
*Photo: Doug Peters/All Action*

Cocking a snook at corporate idiocy at the MTV awards in New York.
*Photo: All Action*

At Jones Beach, Long Island.
One of their last gigs before they flew back to the UK in disarray.
*Photo: All Action*

The coolest mods in the world.
*Photos: Mark Cuthbert/All Action*

Noel and Meg at a
benefit for journalist
Leo Finlay.
*Photo: Suzan Moore
All Action*

A swift half with Paul Weller.
*Photo: John Lillington/All Action*

Noel playing a
surprise solo show
at London's
Mean Fiddler,
21 April '97.
*Photo: Ellis O'Brien
All Action*

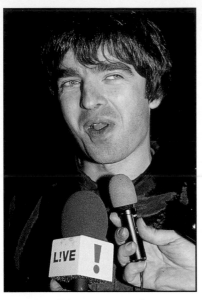

'No comment.'

*Photo: Justin Thomas/All Action*

Noel's new house,
Supernova Heights.

*Photo: Mark Cuthbert/All Action*

Liam on the pitch at his beloved Maine Road.

*Photo: Eamonn Clarke/All Action*

At Oakland Colisseum, 'supporting' U2. World-beaters once more.
*Photos: Pat Pope and Dave Hogan/Rex Features*

At the K-ROQ Weenie Roast in Los Angeles, June '97.
Their first gig in 9 months.

*Photos: All Action*

Liam at San
Francisco's Pan
Pacific hotel.
June '97
'I'm mad for
it again.'

*Photo by Pat Pope*

shtick disappeared roughly two bars into a glorious opening 'Rock & Roll Star'. If anything, their music seemed better suited than ever to a larger auditorium.

There was a barrier roughly halfway back in the crowd to stop anyone getting crushed, but Liam wasn't about to take notice of safety logistics, demanding that anyone who was 'up for it' come down the front. The ensuing rush was like some sort of rock 'n' roll rewrite of the Charge of the Light Brigade.

'I just saw all these people running from everywhere,' Noel recalls, 'and I thought, hey, someone might get killed here if we're not careful. It was scary, but at the same time just about the most exciting thing I'd ever seen in my life. I knew at that moment that we could do everything we ever wanted, everything we'd promised we would.'

The Verve's Richard Ashcroft seemed to agree. Suddenly he popped up next to me by the mixing desk, stood on a podium, looked around at the crowd and yelled, 'THIS IS FUCKING ROCK AND ROLL!!!'

'A lot of us had always had faith in Oasis,' he remembers, 'but I think that was the first moment when I realized just how enormous they were going to be. Of course I was depressed that we hadn't been able to play that night, but I was glad I was there to witness what happened. It was amazing.'

The gig started at full pelt and didn't let up for close to two hours. It also featured the first example of Noel's now regular solo acoustic slots. Perched on a stool, he played a couple of already recorded Oasis songs, then announced, 'This is a new song I wrote in Paris on Tuesday. It's for you, Mathur, 'cos you haven't heard it yet.'

The song was 'Don't Look Back In Anger', the most mature thing Gallagher had yet written. And, sure enough, he'd nicked the Lennon line about 'you said the brains I had went to my head'.

'I told you I would,' he said later.

\*　　\*　　\*

The backstage party found a functional dressing-room converted into what seemed like a Turkish opium den, complete with cloth draped from the ceilings and accompanying music from Oasis's new-found friends the Chemical Brothers. In attendance were a whole host of Gallagher relatives, including their mother, Peggy.

'I was so proud of them that night,' she says. 'I knew they were big and they had a lot of fans, but that night it really showed it. I'd never seen anything like it.'

After an impromptu party at the local Student Union, where people with entrance laminates found themselves beaten up for them outside, some of us adjourned with the band to their hotel, an elegant edifice situated behind electronic gates to stop unnecessary access from the groupies, who were by now more of an annoyance than a bonus.

Everyone in the band seemed ecstatic, apart from Tony.

'That was definitely the end of something,' Bonehead told me at the time. 'And the beginning of something else. I think Tony knew it was the last gig he'd ever play with the band.'

It would be a fortnight before the news broke to the general public, but it was obvious that night that he was right. Tony was out and, with only a fortnight until the release of 'Some Might Say', the record that was to be their first number one, they needed to find a new drummer. And fast.

'Some week, eh?' said Noel.

Yeah, some week.

# 11

## MORNING GLORY

Now they needed a drummer. While Tony McCarroll had always seemed a nice enough bloke, it was becoming obvious that his capabilities weren't going to match the more mature songs that Noel was writing. The animosity between Tony and Liam didn't help and he'd been cast in the role of whipping boy for longer than most people could have endured. While it seemed a little harsh to rob him of a chance to still be officially with the band as they got their first number-one single, there had to be a time for him to leave and, with the recording of the new album due to start almost immediately, there was no time for sentimentality.

And, as Bonehead told the *NME* at the time, they didn't have any hesitation in doing something that was going to make the group better.

'There's no guilt,' he'd insisted. 'If the five of us owned a fish and chip shop and he wasn't putting enough batter on the fish or he weren't frying 'em right or he was burning the chips, then, right, you're sacked.'

The sacking continued to have ramifications for all involved and

131

a lengthy court case initiated by McCarroll for a share of royalties has still not been fully concluded.

Noel wanted a drummer that he thought would be able to do justice to the new songs he'd written, and approached a guy called Alan White, the brother of Paul Weller's drummer, Steve.

'I'd never met him,' says Noel, 'but I'd heard he was good, so I thought, well, I'll meet him and check him out. I had arranged to meet him in this bar in Camden and on the way there I thought, what if he's some ugly thirty-stone bastard? I saw him coming towards me, though, and I thought, thank fuck, he looks normal. So I just said, "Right, mate, you're in." And he's going, "Well, don't you want to hear me play?" I just said, "No, mate, you're not thirty stone, you look all right – do you want the job? Right, now here's a copy of the single. Learn the drums for it and you're doing *Top Of The Tops* with the band tomorrow." It was as easy as that.'

Alan White, born and raised in London, had been drumming for years in various small-time bands (including one called Starclub who made an album that he never actually played on), but never achieved anything like the profile of his brother, who'd been essential to Weller's sound for some years. Nevertheless, Alan's enthusiasm was also accompanied by a very real talent and one which was to make an important contribution to the development of the Oasis sound. Amazingly, despite the rapidity of his audition, he has never been daunted by his role.

'Nah, I mean, the second gig I ever did was at Glastonbury. After that, everything else is a piece of piss.'

White also gives a whole new dynamic to the group. As well as being perfectly capable of drinking and partying along with the best of them, he exudes a sense of quiet stability that reinforces the band's increasing sense of solidity. Plus, he's a cockney, and no part of the Manchester image that has often hindered the band more than it has helped.

Indeed, by early '95, only Bonehead was still living in Manchester.

Guigs and Noel had moved permanently down to London (Noel renting a flat in Camden soon attended every day by gaggles of fans who'd followed him back from the supermarket) and Liam was firmly ensconced in a succession of London hotels.

'I got out of Manchester as soon as I could,' says Noel. 'Everyone there is always trying to find something wrong with what you do. If they ask you to buy them a drink and you don't, they say you're tight. If you do then they call you a flash bastard. You can't win.'

'I was on this train and I wanted to smoke so I was sitting in second class,' says Liam. 'And this woman came up trying to find a seat. She was going, "I want to sit there 'cos I've got like a million children with me," and I said, "Well, you can't, this is my seat." And she goes, "You're a pop star, you're rich, so you should be in first class." If I had been in first class, though, she'd have been, "Well, who does he think he is, showing off sitting there?" What are you supposed to do?'

Not that any of the band actually spent much time in one place, such was the extent of their touring and recording.

In early May, after a triumphant *Top Of The Pops* performance, they headed to the Rockfield studio in Wales for five weeks to record their second album.

Much of the record had already been completed in Noel's head and the title, *(What's The Story) Morning Glory?*, had thankfully ousted the working title of *Flash In The Pan*, so the recording was meant to be an object lesson in speed and simplicity. In fact they did work at a phenomenal rate, averaging a complete song a day and slogging through regular eighteen-hour sessions. Owen Morris was in charge of co-production with Noel, choosing Rockfield, having been banned from the nearby Loco studios for allegedly throwing a chair through a studio window for reasons known only to himself.

'Owen can be sensible most of the time,' says Noel, 'but when he goes for it he's much madder than any of us.'

Within a couple of weeks much of the album had been recorded, including the forthcoming single, 'Roll With It', recorded first take as Noel emerged blearily from a major drinking session.

The band already had some idea of how the record was supposed to sound, having heard Noel play half-written songs to them in the tour bus in Hamburg a few months earlier. He ran through the songs on acoustic guitar, improvising lyrics that hadn't yet been finished, going through the album three or four times. 'Champagne Supernova' had reduced Bonehead to tears and it became clear that *Morning Glory* had the potential to be one of the greatest albums of all time.

As so often before, however, a protracted period of creativity wasn't going to pass by without a swerve towards catastrophe.

That came when Noel arrived back at the studio one night to find Liam hosting a full-scale party.

'There was, like, half of Monmouth in there,' says Noel, 'everyone completely off their faces. I didn't know who any of the people were and they were all just running around the studio. And there's people playing with my guitars, thirty grand's worth of stuff. And that's right out of order. Liam's going, "We're just having a drink," but I wanted them all to fuck off. Some kid comes up to me and asks if I can call a cab for them and I think, right, that's it. Me and our kid got in a fight and I hit him with a cricket bat, then I said, "Can anyone drive?" Alan went, "I can," so I said, "Come on, you're driving me back to London." We were in the middle of making a great record and I could see it completely going off the rails.'

After a week chilling out away from the madness, he returned, forcefully reminding the others that they'd got so close to genuinely colossal success that to throw it away would be the most stupid thing they'd ever do. And they'd done some pretty stupid things in their time.

Finally, at the end of July, the album was cut at – where else?

– Abbey Road studios, and the band prepared for a summer of big-time performances around the country.

First major event was Glastonbury, where they'd been so successful the year before. *En route*, they stopped in Weston-super-Mare to shoot the sleeve for 'Roll With It', posing in front of TV sets with their own personal heroes on each screen.

'It was loosely based on the cover of *With The Beatles*,' designer Brian Cannon explained afterwards. 'And Noel had had a dream about television sets floating down a river, so he said, "Why don't we have TVs in it?"'

That night they played a low-key gig in Bath in preparation for Glastonbury and to give Alan his first taste of playing live with the band. With a whole weekend ahead of them, they peaked far too early, staying up all night and arriving on site the next day looking like they'd just got back from Vietnam.

The Cat in the Hat was there again and many a trip was made to his giant army tent complete with front room and shelving. Evan Dando turned up again: the first time the band had seen him in months. He got so caught up in the relentless pursuit of fun that he turned up for his own performance hours later than advertised, much to the annoyance of promoters and audience alike. Liam appeared equally distracted, winding up reporters by claiming he was going to get married (some of them actually believed him) and observing that Glastonbury was the sort of place, 'where everyone comes along, takes all their clothes off and goes to sit up a tree'. Noel had the cold sweats and insisted on walking around in the blazing heat in a fully toggled-up duffle coat. And a pair of shiny shoes gloriously unsuited to the greenfield site.

'I'm not going anywhere near the mud, man,' he told me. 'Straight from the bar to the stage then on to the bus, that's me. I'm not going to go wandering around with any fucking hippies, thanks very much.'

Instead he spent much of the time with his new best mate,

Robbie Williams, at that time still with Take That. The two hit it off immediately and Robbie was photographed drinking and smoking a spliff. It was to prove both his undoing and salvation.

The gig itself should have been a glorious summer celebration of a band at their very peak playing the biggest gig of their lives. Instead it was largely a scrappy reminder that the band were as capable as anyone else of right royal cock-ups. Two songs in and Liam invited everyone present (all 100,000 of them) up for a fight. One disaffected punter insisted on lobbing two dozen eggs at the stage, although none hit the target. The new songs got caught up in the wind, never delivered with any of the impact that they'd later prove to have. That the whole thing was going out live on Channel 4 didn't help much. The band did manage to turn it around a bit by the end of the set, particularly after Robbie had jumped on stage to dance along.

'When Liam asked him on stage, that was his spiritual calling,' Tim Abbot was reported as saying. 'The puppet strings were cut the day he went on stage.'

'I got my picture in the papers,' says Robbie, 'and when I went to see the others in Take That a few days later, they said they'd had a meeting and they didn't think my behaviour was how someone in the band should behave. That's when they sacked me. I'm glad I did it, though. Meeting Oasis completely changed my attitude to what I was doing and what I wanted to be. It freed me from a lot of things.'

A good day for Robbie perhaps but for the band a major stumble, fuelling the idea that maybe they wouldn't be able to handle the speed and size of their success. Maybe they weren't really as big as their imagination had insisted.

'We just fucked up,' says Noel, 'but I knew we could still do it. I always liked playing the big gigs better than the small ones. I don't like the audience being too close.'

Their next two gigs were under canvas at Irvine Beach in

Scotland. Two successive nights playing to 6,000 people – a time which even now stands out as among the best performances they've ever done.

The rain had lashed down hours before the first night's show, turning the fields around the tent (the largest marquee in the world, on loan from the Chinese State circus) into a muddy approximation of the Somme. The band had chosen support acts with whom they felt they had some affinity and the likes of Cast, the Verve and Smaller went down well in front of a hugely supportive Scottish crowd. Away from Glastonbury and back under a roof, Oasis caught a magic spark from somewhere and, on the first night, played a set that vindicated even the most hyperbolic faith in them. The next night they were even better and as the close of their set segued into DJ Paolo Hewitt playing 'Hey Jude', the band were running around backstage, genuinely moved. Quite why things should have been so different from Glastonbury was something that no one could pinpoint, but it marks out the Oasis live experience. They're either brilliant or shit. Rarely anywhere in between.

'If we were ever just ordinary, that's when I'd start worrying,' says Noel.

After the show the band embarked on a marathon drinking session which ended with Liam punching a ceiling and storming off while Noel conducted an alcoholically crippled interview with Miranda Sawyer, a journalist from the *Observer*.

Still buzzing from the gig earlier and slipping into his most ridiculously cocky mode, he confessed, 'I stare at hotel walls and wonder to myself, where did it go right?' It was when he started ranting about Blur, who'd hinted that they might be releasing their next single directly up against Oasis, that he said something he was to regret for a long time afterwards.

'The guitarist I've got a lot of time for,' he confessed, 'and the drummer, I've never met him, but I hear he's a nice guy. The bass player and the singer – I hope the pair of them get AIDS and die because I fucking hate them.'

Immediately he'd said it, he tried to retract it, but it was too late. When the comment was eventually printed, in September, it seemed to confirm the completely erroneous image of the band as typical Manc homophobes. And by that time the battle between Blur and Oasis would have even made it on to *News At Ten*. Noel's comments weren't about to win any Henry Kissinger peace awards.

In early August Paul Weller played the T In The Park festival and, having had such a good time a year earlier, Noel decided to revisit to hang out with him. He'd checked into the same hotel as me (at that time the Gallagher alias for hotel 'anonymity' was Mr C Supernova!) and when I met him in the foyer he promised to play me an advance tape of the album later. At ten-thirty there was a phone call. 'It's Noel, come down to the lobby now.'

As I got out of the lift, Noel, his girlfriend Meg, Robbie Williams and their friend, the singer Lisa Moorish, were standing by the doors.

'Turn right and keep on walking,' said Noel as we headed towards the back door to the kitchens. A couple of seconds later there was a commotion by the hotel entrance and suddenly we were being chased by a couple of hundred teenage girls who'd all found out that Robbie was in town. Out past the kitchens, over a wall and into a waiting cab, I got to experience just how scary such adulation must be. As we drove off with girls climbing all over the taxi I looked over at Noel. He was grinning.

'Brilliant, isn't it?' he said.

Taking a necessarily circuitous route through the city, we ended up at Lisa Moorish's elegantly discreet hotel and legged it up to her room. After the obligatory lines, Noel got the *Morning Glory* tape out and put it on.

He'd later describe the record as 'like half of it is in a hammock smoking a spliff and the other half's walking around the streets of London with a petrol bomb in its hand'. That night he was content to insist, 'It's the best thing you'll have heard in your life.'

Three quarters of an hour later I was inclined to agree.

Ambivalence is easy. Just as easy as blind faith or amoebic devotion. As a music journalist, I always believed that I, or one of my peers, would stumble across a band that would end up ruling the world. Otherwise, there wouldn't have been much point doing it in the first place. The very first time I heard a tape of Oasis's songs, I genuinely believed that they could be the embodiment of everything I'd ever imagined, could be more than just the apologetically indistinct sketches of the Next Big Thing that the week-long shelf life of my profession demanded. I thought they could be the one.

A couple of minutes later, I made half-heartedly for the security of a carefully considered reaction. I instinctively tried to convince myself that they could instead be just flashy novelties, and that the effect they had on my life said more about my own lunge towards a justification for what I did than any inherent excellence they might have possessed. They sounded like the best thing I had heard in my life, but could they really be so important?

Of course they could. And the first time I saw them rehearse, the first night I hung out with them, I was struck by the strength of their all-consuming self-confidence. They didn't seem to have any space in their world for the prospect of failure.

I wrote some words in the music press, had lots of inspiring conversations, told everyone I knew that they were something different, something special.

Somewhere deep down, though, there was still a tiny doubt, a nagging feeling that I'd drifted imperceptibly into some dopily self-possessed proclamation of excellence.

There's a mundanely cynical chasm that separates hope from accomplishment and, just occasionally, I wondered whether I'd end up haplessly treading water, trying not to drown in a torrentially daft defence of mediocrity. Sure, there'd been great moments so far, apparent confirmations that Oasis were every bit as good as I'd originally thought. But what if it all fell apart now? What if they were to implode, remembered only as one-album wonders? What if it stopped just before it could begin big time? I understood how easily enthusiasm could be interpreted as a glib, misguided celebration of some sort of fractured perception of brilliance. I knew I could end up looking like the loopily intransigent loser who hangs around at last orders, defending the good old days through the haze of a selectively rewritten past. It's easy to be wrong.

And it's a lot harder to be right.

Two songs into the tape of *Morning Glory*, any doubts were finally obliterated, drenched by the power of what cascaded out of the speakers, by songs of a quality that even Oasis had only hinted at before. I was dumbfounded.

Before that bit of that night, my favourite albums of all time had been *Don't Stand Me Down* by Dexy's Midnight Runners, *Rubber Soul* and *Revolver* by the Beatles, *Fire Escape In The Sky* by Scott Walker and *Setting Sons* by the Jam. Afterwards, everything but Dexy's got bumped down a place.

And I knew that Oasis hadn't been hurling out any false promises. They'd made a record that torched any doubts, vindicated all those hours spent defending them to friends who'd dismissed them as dreary retro-merchants.

After the tape ended, my grumbling – 'You're a bastard, you've done it again' – seemed to be even more annoyingly unnecessary. It's always a give-away when a room full of people on coke are reduced to silence.

'What do you think?' asked Noel, coming over all rhetorical.

After he'd disentangled himself from the speechless hugs, he played it again.

Usually, when a rock star talks you through their new album, you don't even need to explain why you're getting a cab off to somewhere a long way away to watch some concrete set. When it's Noel, you have to hang around, getting almost as much entertainment between the tracks as inside the grooves.

So, that night, as he played *Morning Glory* again, he anticipated every twist in the plot, pointing out loads of the bits that he'd nicked, showing how he'd flipped the individual elements into something brand-new.

One of the tracks on the original tape was called 'Step Out'.

'This is "Uptight" by Stevie Wonder and "Rosalee" by Thin Lizzy,' he boasted. 'In the same song!!!' Before the eventual release, Stevie would run his fingers over a report in Braille of Noel's comment, deciding that there was nothing big or clever about a British rock 'n' roll group paying tribute to his genius and managing to come up with a Heavy Metal Northern Soul classic. He'd ask for ridiculously excessive royalties and Oasis would drop the track from the album, putting it on the B-side of a single and sending him a cheque for a few thousand quid. Gary Glitter, on the other hand, would negotiate a deal for the bit of one of his songs that they used on 'Hello', mentioning that he was flattered that a band like Oasis were reminding people of his past glories. The song would remain on the album and his cheques keep rolling in to this day. Make of it what you will. And remember, this decade's watchword is 'doh!!!'

As Noel talked his way through the album, he explained the inspiration behind some of the words and tunes. 'She's Electric' drew on the theme from a kids' television show. 'Cast No Shadow' was a supportive nod to his mate, the prodigiously gifted Richard Ashcroft from the Verve, particularly his '94 gig at Glastonbury. 'Wonderwall' was about Meg, the only girl he'd met who came close to being as important as his music and the one who understood him better than almost anyone else. The instrumental bits used to be called 'The Jam', but he dropped the name because he thought

Paul Weller would be offended, then, when it was all too late to change it, Weller told him he should have kept the original title because it was funny.

And 'Don't Look Back In Anger'? Of course he'd nicked the Lennon line from that night in Paris. And if you couldn't spot the piano bit from 'Imagine' at the beginning, you couldn't really have been listening properly. There was another reference, though. The lines that demanded, 'Stand up beside the fireplace/Take that look from off your face', were dredged from memories of the family photo that Noel, Liam and Paul would endure every Christmas. That Peggy's insistence that her sons stop fidgeting would end up as a line on a number one record should be a source of inspiration to everyone, everywhere.

Oh, and to squash any head-scratching theories, Noel did sign an autograph in a cab for the driver's daughter, who was beside herself at (erroneous) reports that Oasis were about to split up. And she was called Sally. But the 'Sally' of the song doesn't exist. Never has. Never will. Just words. Live with it.

After we'd forced Noel to play the tape of the album a dozen times, Robbie and I headed down to the bar. He opened up about his frustration with Take That, admitting that he'd been writing poems and lyrics of his own for years. I dumbly expected sixth-form demonstrations of deficiency, but when he started reciting some of his words, I was blown away. Few of the lyrics he revealed that night will ever be incorporated into any of his songs, primarily because many of them were fuelled by a bitterness and insecurity directly related to his recent exit from Take That, but they were packed with smart, surprisingly memorable lines that belied his teenybop image. They seemed far more suited to the kind of music being made by Oasis and their contemporaries. I told him as much in the corridor outside the hotel room and drunkenly threatened to recite as much as I could remember to Noel once we staggered back inside.

'You can't,' protested Robbie. 'He's a proper songwriter and everything. What if he thinks what I've written is a load of shit?'

Inside, I said to Noel, 'You should hear Robbie's lyrics. They're brilliant. There's one that goes . . .'

'OK,' said Robbie, and he read out half a dozen of his 'songs'.

When he'd finished, Noel stayed quiet. I started to wonder whether he was too far gone to have even taken in anything Robbie had said. Or whether I'd been wrong and it had all been a load of old bollocks.

'If you don't put those out in a year,' said Noel, 'I'm having them. They're fucking great, man.'

Back at my hotel, Robbie, Noel, Lisa and Meg kept the party going. As we'd got in the lift up to the room, a girl who couldn't have been more than thirteen had burst through the security cordon. She stood in front of Robbie and said, 'You betrayed the band, you cunt. You're dead.' It was one of the most disorientatingly disturbing moments of my life, a snapshot of success turned inside out and squeezed into a nasty new weapon.

Robbie Williams, now very much ex-Take That, gave her the finger.

A couple of hours later, our cigarette-smoke-filled room triggered off fire alarms all over the hotel, causing everyone else to be evacuated. The manager came into the room, clocked Robbie, unscrewed the smoke alarm, told him it was OK and apologized for causing any inconvenience. The pop-star perks seemed to just about make up for the wrath of disgruntled fans delivering pubescent death threats.

At one point Robbie was talking about how he hadn't had a day off since he was sixteen. Five years of people telling him what he was supposed to do. Now he'd been kicked out of Take That, he felt robbed of confidence, convinced that anyone who'd ever rated him would soon forget that he'd ever existed. The *Daily Star*'s sanctimonious, hypocritical 'revelations' about Robbie's lifestyle and his behaviour at T In The Park only contributed to his lack of self-confidence.

I told him he should start to enjoy himself, asking him how much money he had in the bank.

'I don't know exactly,' he said to me. 'Gary [Barlow, Take That's songwriter] has got loads more than the rest of us. I think, in the bank, I've got about a million.'

'Shit,' said Noel, the man who'd done nothing but enjoy himself for the last couple of years. 'I haven't even got a tenth of that.'

Within a year, a costly court case would leave Robbie almost penniless. And Noel would have more millions than fingers. Pop 'n' roll shifts shape faster than you could ever imagine.

'The court case cost a lot of money,' says Robbie, 'but I'm glad I'm doing what I'm doing now. I was dead scared the first time I met Oasis and when I was at T In The Park. I thought all the indie bands would think I was just some superficial plastic pop star. I needed to get some confidence back and I got it off that weekend. Then and at Glastonbury, I got the chance to have a good time and to realize what I wanted to do. After Take That I'd been told that I was nothing, and I'd begun to believe it. You hang around Noel and Liam, though, and they're really supportive. They were the ones that made me think, yeah, fuck it, I can do something. Have they been an inspiration? Of course they have.'

'He's a nice bloke,' says Noel, describing Robbie. 'And he's got the right attitude. But he's not joining the band, no matter what rumours you might hear. Top geezer, though.'

# 12

---

# HELP IN ABBEY ROAD

As Oasis's success continued to soar into the realms of unreality, their shows got ever bigger. And while they usually headlined, they did play a few gigs supporting R.E.M., the group who, within months, they leapfrogged to the title of the World's Best Selling Rock Group. Oasis had already turned down offers of support slots from the likes of the Stones, David Bowie and Bon Jovi, but since R.E.M. were fans and their musical constituency inevitably overlapped with that of Oasis, the support slot seemed a sensible option.

And the gigs went well, climaxing in a massive outdoor show at Slane Castle, near Dublin, in July. Ten months after their last visit to Ireland, it was a booking that came with all the big-time comforts calculated to smooth out any mundane aggravations surrounding anything but the show itself. Oasis arrived by helicopter and at once set about taking advantage of the plentiful booze that filled a luxurious backstage complex. The confidence was back and so were many of their relatives, including their mum and elder brother. And they weren't to be disappointed as Oasis turned in a dynamic, assured performance that finally confirmed they could handle even the largest of venues.

Afterwards, as almost everyone had come to expect, things went briefly pear-shaped. Traffic jams around the area meant that the band had to hang around for hours and, as frustration kicked in, niggly little arguments escalated into a full-scale fight, taking some of the sheen off what should have been the definitive moment in Oasis's assertion of greatness.

The fights were not a surprise. What was a shock, though, was sound man Mark Coyle's decision to quit. Over recent shows he'd felt his hearing going and, afraid that it would pack up all together, he decided that Slane Castle would be his last show.

His decision came as a complete surprise to the rest of the band and they tried, in vain, to make him change his mind. Not only was his experience and understanding a guarantee that Oasis could make their live performances as effective as they always intended, but he'd also become an integral part of the whole entourage, one of the veterans who'd been with them right since the early days. It would take some time to get used to his not being around and his immediate replacement, Robbie McGrath, was given a hard time when he tried to step into Coyle's shoes. Things were changing and, it seemed, not always for the better.

More frustration was to come with the release of Oasis's seventh single, 'Roll With It'. Noel had decided that he wanted to achieve four successive number ones to match Paul Weller's achievement with the Jam and, after 'Some Might Say', had high hopes that the follow-up would top the singles charts without too much difficulty.

The song itself was no classic, although its straightforward rock 'n' roll impulse combined with yet another example of Noel's facility for writing tunes that worked their way into your head within half a dozen hearings. At the time of its conception it seemed a dead cert for number-one status.

\*　　\*　　\*

Nineteen ninety-five was the Summer of Britpop. A rediscovered public affection for guitar music, something unquestionably triggered by Oasis themselves, had lead to a host of groups moving out of the ghetto of the indie charts and into the mainstream. In recent years such a crossover had only been achieved by the flourishing dance scene and it was common to see records moving within weeks from 'underground' club status to the higher reaches of the charts.

Guitar rock was a different matter. By its very nature it had remained peripheralized, at times determinedly so, as if to court widespread appeal would be to betray its self-perceived authenticity. Oh, and half the time its protagonists seemed scared shitless of being anything other than big fish in a small, muddy pond. Oasis's bold refusal to subscribe to such small-mindedness had provided many of their contemporaries with a blueprint for something more ambitious and created an environment where the genre that they embrace could flourish.

Bands like Blur and Pulp had reiterated the potential of conventionally structured pop, unashamedly influenced by acts like the Kinks, the Small Faces and, of course, the Beatles. Blur's *Parklife* album and 'Girls & Boys' single had given them a whole new fan base, people who would never read the weekly music press and who put their records on their shelves next to Kylie Minogue and Boyzone. Despite the snobbery of indie purists, the changing face of British pop was the healthiest thing that had happened to this nation's music in years and, when acts like Cast, the Bluetones and Supergrass found their records appreciated by a whole new audience, the Britpop tag started to be pinned to any young chancers with trainers and guitars. And the media and industry imposed sobriquet often seemed more debilitating than constructive. Nevertheless, it ensured that, with Blur and Oasis both due to release singles around the same time, the rivalry between the two bands was thrown into even sharper focus.

Relations between the two hadn't improved since an afternoon at a San Francisco radio station the previous year, a couple of days before the disastrous Whiskey A Go-Go gig. Introduced to each other on air, Damon had called Liam a 'geezer'. Gallagher had responded with 'wanker' and while he'd confessed to actually liking some of *Parklife*, the atmosphere between the two never came close to anything resembling friendship.

In the meantime, whenever they'd met, snide comments had been the order of the day, invariably initiated by Oasis. It had to come to a head, and in August, it did.

Blur had originally intended to release their single towards the end of the month, just ahead of the release of their 'Great Escape' album, expecting Oasis to put something out a few weeks afterwards. When, however, 'Roll With It' was scheduled for release on 14 August, Blur decided to put their single out the same week in direct competition. And the whole affair degenerated into a ludicrous competition between the two that may have garnered a lot of media coverage (even making *News At Ten*) but which dragged both groups into an undignified slanging match. People in the Creation camp tried to interpret the whole affair as some sort of daft class war, whereas Blur weren't any less cock-eyed in resorting to accusations that Oasis were just a nineties version of Status Quo. Radio DJ Chris Evans played 'Roll With It' over the phone to Blur's Damon Albarn in a hotel room in Glasgow and Albarn responded by singing Quo's 'Rockin' All Over The World' over the top of it. Oasis immediately put out their own T-shirts emblazoned with the word 'Quoasis'.

When, on 14 August, the two singles were released head to head, the whole thing merely served to emphasize the manipulative vagaries of chart-assault marketing. Oasis had a larger fan base than Blur and were expected to just beat their rivals to the top, both groups long having realized that, whatever the outcome, the two records would enter the charts straight at number one and number two. When the result was finally revealed though, Blur were in the top spot. And the recriminations started.

Rumours had suggested that Oasis's position was due to a misprinting of bar-codes on the sleeve of the single, resulting in sales to chart-return shops not actually being registered. But in fact Blur had got to number one simply by releasing their single in a variety of different formats, including two CDs with different bonus tracks. The fans therefore would have to buy two copies.

No one had explained this to the band, however, and Noel's first response was anger at what he regarded as Creation's ineptitude.

When Marcus Russell had asked him, 'Who do they think they [Creation] are?', Noel had replied, 'No, who do they think WE are?', going on to publicly berate the label for using their success to merely bankroll indulgent side-projects.

'I was really concerned that Noel had this idea that it was all our fault, and that we were acting like amateurs,' says Alan McGee, 'so I went down to see him in the studio. I said to him, "How do you feel?" And he went, "How do you think I feel? I feel like number two, man." It was obvious he was really pissed off with us. After I'd told him about the whole format thing, though, I think he realized that it wasn't our fault. I don't think anyone came out of that whole Blur v Oasis thing very well. But if anyone started it all it was Blur.'

Still angry, Noel went out on a three-day bender with Paul Weller before turning up with the band at *Top Of The Pops* for the consolation 'Roll With It' appearance. As a somewhat petulant, if understandably defiant gesture, Noel then insisted that everyone swap instruments for the performance, miming to the vocals while Liam pretended to play guitar.

And the animosity between Oasis and Blur continued, this time primarily due to a piece of potentially dangerous brinkmanship on Blur's behalf.

Oasis had scheduled a short British tour for September that included a date in Bournemouth. Blur at once announced that they were also going to play Bournemouth. On the same night, and across the road from the International Centre where Oasis were due to play. There was even talk of them projecting Blur logos on to the front of the Centre, an inflammatory gesture that raised fears of the whole night devolving into a giant fight.

'It would have ended up just being full of hooligans turning up for a scrap,' says Johnny Hopkins. 'Blur were just being really stupid again.'

'I hate Blur,' says Noel, 'but I know we've got fans who like them and if they'd bought tickets for our show that night, they wouldn't have been able to see them. Blur were just trying to do something to piss us off and they didn't even care about their own fans. That says a lot about them.'

Determined not to be drawn any further into a stand-off that they felt anyway would be settled when *Morning Glory* was released, Oasis postponed their British tour, Bournemouth date included, until October. There was a feeling within the Oasis camp that there was going to have to be a time soon to down-scale the touring. A forthcoming American jaunt had already brought up enquiries from a couple of promoters as to whether the band would actually turn up. Fate and the inevitable chaos that accompanied previous American tours had meant that the band had already twice cancelled gigs in St Louis, and organizers didn't want to get burned again. Plus, the band themselves had spent much of the last two years on the road and come dangerously close to self-combustion. They were too close to what they'd always wanted to throw it all away.

Nevertheless, a decision was made to carry on for the next few months at least, starting with a short tour of Japan. Management reasoned, sensibly, that the draconian drug laws in Japan would ensure a relatively 'clean' week and, of course, a chance for the band to consolidate their success in that territory.

Having heard about the hysterical response to the band's last visit to Japan, an old friend of theirs, Sid Cox, had decided to go out with them. Sid had been ever-present at loads of Oasis shows over the past three years, and was a good mate and drinking buddy of Liam's. He was also one of the few who has never asked or expected anything of them other than the continual mutual appreciation of the pursuit of a good time.

Unable to afford the flight to Tokyo on the same airline as Oasis, he bought a cheap ticket on Aeroflot, figuring it was worth the risk of trusting his life to a flying cattle shed if the wildness of Japan was going to live up to all the things he'd heard. And to finance his time out there, he came up with an audacious entrepreneurial plan. Having heard that Japanese fans were obsessively well informed about all things Oasis, regularly turning up to gigs in Manchester City football shirts, he decided to get in on the action. Back in Manchester he bought a hundred Man City key fobs and, when he reached Tokyo, persuaded the merchandisers to put them alongside the Oasis T-shirts on sale at every gig. And, figuring rightly that if the Japanese really want something they'll pay as much as you ask, he put them up for sale for a tenner a piece. £990 clear profit. Party money.

And it was a good job he had it, because the band spent the week taking every opportunity to indulge the intoxicating opportunities that accompanied their Oriental superstar status. Since they were trapped for much of the time in the Ropongi Prince Hotel in Tokyo, their every journey outside the front door to buy Beatles rarities or investigate brand-new favourite bars was accompanied by the kind of crowd scenes you'd expect to see at some sort of state occasion. The gigs themselves were scenes of mass hysteria that startled even the cynical observers who'd noted that any even half-decent band can expect an adulation in Japan far in excess of any objective worth. Oasis's seven gigs sold out in hours and the fans were only too happy to oblige the band's every whim, which included a narcotic supplement to the endless drinking. By the end of the week Liam's voice was shot to pieces and sleep deprivation had kicked in all round. Any ideas that the tour was to have been like some sort of trip to a health farm had gone out of the window pretty much as soon as they arrived. By the time they were swimming naked in the hotel pool on their last night in Tokyo, the strain of a forthcoming American tour seemed like it could easily tear them apart.

The fears were to prove at least partly right, but such was the freneticism of their activity that no one had much time for self-analysis. They had the wind behind them and they were hurtling at horizons.

On 5 September, Noel went into Abbey Road Studios to record an acoustic version of 'Fade Away' with friends Lisa Moorish and the actor Johnny Depp for the charity album *Help*. Artists all over the country were recording in studios on that day, the aim being to gather together all the tracks and have a finished album out within the week, all profits to go to help the people of Bosnia.

Tony Crean was the man with the original idea for the album – something that seemed all the more admirable coming as it did after the shabbiness of the Blur-Oasis saga. The whole thing depended completely on that rarest of concepts, pop stars putting their egos on the back burner in the cause of something greater than their own self-serving obstinacy. And, to their credit, all the acts involved did justice to the nobility of Crean's vision, the album ultimately raising enough money to make a very real difference to the lives of a lot of Bosnians and doing much to restore some sort of worth to the character of the Great British Rock Star.

'There was an amazing atmosphere in Abbey Road,' says Crean. 'Everyone was genuinely really into the whole project, and you were never sure quite what was going to happen, or who was going to turn up. You got the feeling that something really special was happening.'

Paul Weller was due to record a track, and asked Noel to help out. The two already had a history of working together that went back to Weller's previous *Stanley Road* album, when Noel had played guitar on a cover version of Dr John's 'Walk on Gilded Splinters'.

'I was just hanging out with him when he was doing that album,' says Noel, 'and he said, "Do you know this Dr John song?" I was, like, "Yeah, course I do", so he started playing and I joined in. Afterwards, he goes, "You've never heard that before in your life, have you?" and he'd realized that I'd been bluffing the whole thing. He still used it, though, and I went away thinking, yeah, I played on a Weller album!!! I know it didn't make any difference to the sales, but it was good to know that I'd done it.'

Liam had previously done uncredited handclaps on the Verve's *A Northern Soul* album and he and Noel looked back on the experience with a sense of satisfaction at what they'd done with people they genuinely believed in rather than any sort of self-centred boasting. As glib as it might look in print, anyone who knows them will confirm that no matter how much success comes their way, and no matter that they're consistently capable of acting like complete dickheads, there's always a genuine faith in something bigger that motivates and inspires them. A love of music and an affinity with those that share a belief in its eternal importance. It's a thin line between such an attitude and the dull muso value system that shackles any attempts at originality. And it's that thin line that has made so many critics despise a puritanism that they feel Oasis and their peers will always embody. They may be right. But I doubt it.

Paul Weller played on *Morning Glory*, further emphasizing the bond between him and Noel. As well as harmonica on 'Swamp Song', he also threw in guitar, harmonica and backing vocals on 'Champagne Supernova', the track that Noel had conceived as a 'Stairway To Heaven' for the nineties, 'without all the elves and cosmic shite'.

'It was weird when I started to get friends with him and we hung out together,' says Noel. 'He'd be sitting there all night while I asked him millions of questions about the Jam. If anyone had told me five years ago that I'd be friends with him and playing on one of his albums, I'd have been, "Yeah, right, fuck off."'

At Abbey Road, though, his wildest dreams were just about to come sashaying in.

'Fade Away' was finished quickly and the collaboration with Weller was underway. As befitting the location, a plan was made to do a cover of the Beatles' 'Come Together', a song both suited to the loose, easy feel of the collaboration and resonant title-wise with the motive behind the album. Suddenly, the doors opened and in came Paul McCartney with his wife Linda, ready to play. And so, under the banner Mojo Filters, the pictures on Gallagher's bedroom wall all those years before came down to give him a smile he still hasn't entirely wiped off his face.

# 13

## GUIGS CHILLS

Where would any randomly selected segment from the Oasis narrative be without a crisis breaking and entering a bit where it all seemed to be going so well? Unless you'd been one of the people close enough to them to seriously care about their future, one of the people who've constantly had to engage in damage limitation and bleary, late-night solutions to a career that could easily have crumpled before the level-headedness of the cold light of day, you might well have whooped at Oasis's unerring grasp of dramatic self-possession. The big 'but' has always managed to elbow its way past any illusions of infallibility, often, in retrospect at least, a warranted reminder that they'd only get everything they ever wanted if they started to remember just why they'd wanted it in the first place.

There'd been some big problems before, plenty of times when you couldn't have blamed them for jacking it all in, retreating with the royalties until the money ran out, happy at least that the grim nights driving a minicab could be whiled away with a bunch of brilliant memories. By the summer of '95 they'd already made a difference, ensured an archival immortality. It might have been enough for another 50p on the tips.

And, with each successive threat to their continuity somehow overcome, there was at least the consolation that the offers for the rights to the TV movie were exponentially expanding.

All credit to people like Marcus Russell, Tim Abbot and, indeed, the post-tired-and-emotional incarnations of Oasis for keeping things going, but by the time the band geared up to launch the *Morning Glory* album, I'm sure I wasn't alone in losing patience with a seemingly pathological intention within the band to throw it all away. One minute they had it all, the next they had got tangled in a mishap of their own making. You felt that if they were going to be remembered as an adjunct to a pile of twisted metal, it ought to at least end with a light aircraft slamming into a mountainside, not a creaky shopping trolley careering into a pile of cans of cut-price baked beans.

On their return from Japan they were obliged to hawk their forthcoming product in various European cities and, by the time they reached Paris, the wheels that had spent so long trying to control a joyride around the global car park finally came loose, rolling off the wagon and into the nearest ditch.

A live interview at a Parisian radio station had been ruined when Liam decided that having comedian Eddie Izzard was some sort of slight on a perceived notion of Oasis as all-conquering. He walked out and ended up getting punched by the band's tour manager, Ian Robertson. As the night wore on and drink made straight for the stomach, bypassing any acknowledgement of the past, the future or, to be honest, any bit of the world that existed between big mouth and fuzzy logic, Liam got stroppier than ever, laying into Guigs for something that only the ice cubes in the triple shot of JD will ever know.

It's easy to set up Liam as the band's loose cannon, the one who always seems to be at the centre of situations that later on, much later on, someone is going to realize will take some explaining. To trace him as some sort of deranged liability. Try such instinctive generalizations as that and I know I wouldn't be the only one to leap into the queue to defend him to the death.

Liam Gallagher is, by some distance, the most complex person I know. And also the most spiritual, the only person I know whose soul twitches beneath the deceptive swagger of his bluff public persona. While he is undeniably guilty of regularly shitty behaviour, he is precociously aware of life's thunderously intangible subtleties. His headlong barrelling into a celebration of life all too often muddles the initial impulse, concentrates on the fact that he's done the lines rather than appreciating that he spotted the sparkles between them as well.

He goes for it, vindicated by his youth and an acknowledgement from those within a worldwide radius around him that he's an iconic personification of the classic rock 'n' roll star. And, when he's wrong, you can't expect him to admit it until the speedway inside his head has slowed sufficiently to reveal the world outside as more than just an impressionistic blur.

Guigs had seen it all before. He knew what Liam was like and understood that words were just words. He'd been through the hangover post-mortem where no one brought up the vicious insults and the mental bruises were just a side-dish for the territory. He wasn't some emotional weakling.

That night in Paris, though, as the insults arced over with their usual haphazard persistence, he had suddenly felt that maybe he couldn't put up with it any more. There was a weariness he had not previously experienced, a fast-forward flash about having to go through it all again, night after night on a twelve-berth tour capsule, dragging itself across America's highways.

He pulled out of the next day's interviews and asked for a ticket straight back to London to be booked.

A few days later Oasis told the world that Guigs had left the group for a bit because of nervous exhaustion. He'd be missing from the forthcoming British and American tours while he sorted himself out.

'At first I thought it would be a real relief,' says Guigs, 'but then I got home and just hung around. And it was the most boring time of my life. I knew I was going to go back.'

The rest of the band knew as well, or at least maintained, to themselves as much as anyone else, that his absence was only temporary. Over the past year they'd been playing bigger and bigger gigs, the required entourage throwing up more and more faces they'd never seen before. Tony's dismissal was inevitable. Mark Coyle's farewell was just about bearable. Guigs, though, that was different. He'd be back. He had to be. No one wanted to think any further.

In the meantime the band had to draft in a replacement, and someone came up with the name of Scott McLeod, bassist with a Manchester band called the Ya Ya's, a group advised by former Stone Roses manager Gareth Evans. McLeod's technical ability was of less concern than the fact that his appointment would keep things within a group of people that they knew. With Tony it was easy to admit that he was never coming back, and confidently acknowledge his replacement. Guigs wasn't out, though. He was just chilling for a bit. And Scott, no matter how talented he may have been, was never being offered a permanent position.

Gareth Evans told McLeod to take the offer or regret it for ever.

Scott said yes.

'We're going to take a picture of him,' said Noel. 'A before-and-after. Just to see how much he ages, and how quick.'

As he arrived at Euston station with a couple of the band, ready for rehearsals, Scott McLeod was met with a barricade of paparazzi.

'Is it always like this?' he asked, visibly shocked at the flashbulb attention.

'No,' said Noel. 'It's worse.'

The problems within the band may have seemed important to them, but the kids down at Woolworth's were more concerned with something else.

As with *Definitely Maybe*, there was a triple-jump-type distance between the inception of the songs on *Morning Glory* and their eventual release. The band had played a few of the songs live, and bootlegs of five or six cuts had found their way, as they always must, on to the odd sixth-generation tape. In my dotage I might just regret not selling anyone the tape that, over the couple of months, I'd resisted tabloid offers for. To be honest, I won't. As much as the band, I was fascinated by the prospect of an audience full of hopes, dreams, prejudice and preconceptions faced with an album that would always be the Technicolor to the retrospectively relative monochrome of *Definitely Maybe*. I wanted to hear the collective gasp just as much as the band did.

Halfway through the band's chaotic '95 American tour I'd been offered money by a Sunday tabloid to spill the beans on the exact extent of Oasis's chiselling away at US narcotics regulations and took great pleasure in ringing up the paper's editor, laboriously negotiating a ridiculously convoluted cash deal and then saying, 'Oh, by the way, fuck off, I don't snitch on my mates.' It was an easy decision to make and one that I knew I'd never regret, even if I'd been offered a million dollars.

The backhander for the tape of the album was a proposition much harder to resist. I wouldn't be betraying people I cared about, other than to gazump one of the other half-dozen people who'd got the tape that were undoubtedly on the tabloid's bounty-hunting list. And those songs. They were something else. Maybe I owed it to the world to let them loose.

'It's me again,' I told the editor.

'Hey, hi!'

'Fuck right off.'

Anticipation had to be everything. Unless, as it turned out, you were writing about the album for the music press.

Initial reviews were bewilderingly lukewarm, most of the writers expressing disappointment that *Morning Glory* wasn't simply a rewrite of *Definitely Maybe*. There were suggestions that the band were out of their depth trying to do anything other than straight-forward ramalamarock, and that in trying to expand their sound they'd dissipated their strength. *Morning Glory* was dismissed as merely ordinary.

I'd spent over a decade as a music journalist, deflecting what seemed like unfair accusations about how our only relationship with bands was to build 'em up and knock 'em down, apparently reporting regularly to a cabal that existed only to whimsically clatter into any act that looked like getting a momentum of its own. Indeed, I still write for *Melody Maker* and no matter how much I try to communicate an enthusiasm for music that affects me, maybe even me alone, but certainly detached from any perceived party line, I still get missives from disaffected readers, demanding in green crayon that I prostrate myself in front of some sort of consensual definition of greatness. An entity that, as they conveniently forget to mention, would never have existed in the first place without the poorly paid, naively idealistic writers from the very paper they're complaining about who championed them from the start.

I wasn't about to start swapping shirts with the ranks of the misguidedly self-righteous.

But, those reviews of *Morning Glory*. They were wrong. What were the music hacks thinking of? I'll tell you what they were doing. They were just building 'em up to knock 'em down. They must have been listening to the wrong record.

Oops.

Journalists are never going to admit to mistakes, preferring to bandy around words like 'reappraisal' and 'premature', many of them confessing now that their disappointment with the album came more from their expectations about what the follow-up to *Definitely Maybe* should sound like than a blanket disappointment with the songs that *Morning Glory* revealed. As someone never really sure on which side of the fence I should be standing, I tried to defend both the criticisms and the accolades, but, deep down, I know where my instinctive allegiance lies. Call me a quisling and give me that light for that Molotov. The press were wrong.

Despite the reviews, advance information suggested that the album would go straight into the album charts at number one. What wasn't anticipated was the sheer volume of sales. Within four days of release it had sold almost a quarter of a million copies and by the end of the week had notched up 346,000, the best first-week figures in eight years and only 4,000 short of the all-time record held by Michael Jackson's album *Bad*. By the end of the year it would have sold over 1,750,000 copies and, by the summer of '96 it had gone platinum nine times over, marking over five million copies sold.

The record's release meant a lot to everyone involved and no one was about to let the first day of its availability pass by unacknowledged. So, on the morning of Sunday 1 October, a hundred of Oasis's closest friends gathered at a louchely ornate gentlemen's club in Pavilion Road in London's Knightsbridge, ready to warm up for an all-day assertion of a trust in the belief of the only people that mattered: the fans who would go out and buy the record. At midnight, they would play a gig at the Virgin Megastore in Oxford Street, in front of a couple of hundred of the people who'd ultimately be the first to decide whether there was still any point in the band proclaiming any superlative intent. It was eleven in the morning and the offer of free champagne before the sun even thought about clambering over the yard arm was always going to be a fizzy prelude to a symphony of possibilities.

Literally so, since, across the room from an ice sculpture in the shape of the Oasis logo, a string quartet called Pure Strings played an instrumental version of the whole of *Morning Glory*.

'That shows they're good songs,' said Noel as I vainly tried to convince myself that the mushrooms and scrambled eggs on offer were clinically proven to line the stomach. 'Even "She's Electric" sounds good on a violin.'

'They do work well,' confirmed Pure Strings' Stephen Hussey, the man who'd arranged all the tunes. 'Noel can't read or write music, but he's got a good sense of how to construct a song.'

A couple of hours later Liam strode into the toilet with me, unbelievably managing to pull off the sartorial decision to wear a white mackintosh like Harold Wilson used to sport.

'We should get them to put that whole instrumental thing out,' he said. 'We could put a tape out free with a single or something. It'd be brilliant. I'm up for it.'

To date Oasis have not seriously championed such an enterprise, but the string version of the album should be heard by anyone who doubts the proficiency that underpins the band's songs. 'It could be on Radio 2,' I remarked to Noel, failing to anticipate that the official version of 'Wonderwall' would get almost as much airplay on that station as it did on the youth-friendly Radio 1. You may not have approved of it, but you couldn't fail to admit that *Morning Glory* was the most assertively melodic rock album to be released in years.

All very well, but by early afternoon musical appreciation was getting to be an afterthought. Noel headed off back home along with his mum, leaving Ed, photographer Tom Sheehan's permanently-on-call driver, to drive him, me, Liam and Brian Cannon to Camden to watch Cantona's comeback for Man United against Liverpool. During the drive, even kids in the car next to us recognized Liam, a reminder that the band had gone way beyond the comprehensible impression of being just music-press darlings, identifiable to someone who couldn't even scrawl the words '*Melody Maker*' in joined-up writing, let alone appreciate anything that it had unveiled.

As we lurched out of the cab across from Camden's Parkway bar, Liam decided to question everyone he bumped into about the long-term value of Stuart Hall as first-choice presenter of TV's *It's A Knockout*, marvellously, if unintentionally, completely disarming anyone who might have been about to ask for an autograph.

Inside, Noel and Peggy had already found themselves a place in a corner, politely fielding any intrusions. Liam, meanwhile, was the very soul of friendliness, happy to chat with anyone who stumbled his way. As a Liverpool fan, I was glad to have been assured of his support, even by default, the Red Scum being as hated by City fans as by Liverpool supporters. United scraped a draw, thanks to a lucky penalty, but Liam and Noel remained stoically unperturbed. And they ducked in, a couple of hours later, to the Heavenly Sunday Social in Smithfield's, London's meat-market-based hootenanny and the club where the Chemical Brothers had first shown Noel their appreciation of Oasis's music. That despite the fact that the first time I'd taken him down, he'd found himself forced to exchange handshakes with them over the noxious cloud of a spilt bottle of poppers. Every Oasis representative present insisted on inviting anyone who felt like it to the band's Virgin Megastore gig, guaranteeing the presence an hour or so later of at least fifty people, wondering how to fully explain the reason for loitering around a back door in a West End side-street while jerking along to trace memories of rhythmic anthems played earlier. The ones who got in soon made it clear that they didn't have a clue where they were or why they'd turned up in the first place, giving the game away by making straight for the Star Trek lifts and heading up to the top floor to fall over, grappling anything with a pulse as they toppled to the ground.

Downstairs, Oasis weren't exactly flying any flag for sobriety.

A short set was meant to include some songs from the new

album, but when Noel bet Liam fifty quid that he couldn't remember complete versions of any of the new stuff, you couldn't help feeling nervy. Especially when you knew that none of the people on stage (Noel, Liam and Alan) had been entirely comfortable with the idea of even standing upright only moments earlier.

It was a shambles, but a good-natured, sporadically wonderful shambles for all that. And the band were only too keen to sign autographs for the seemingly endless lines of people who waited to the end. Oddly enough, a day that seemed to be gagging for the predictability of ragged chaos, turned out to be a cocky demonstration of Oasis's ability to vault the most imposing of obstacles.

It was just the little ones that continued to clip their heels.

Hours after the Megastore appearance, they headed off on four British dates, including the postponed Bournemouth gig. Scott seemed to be doing all right, the others deliberately convincing themselves that he was only going to be a proficient short-term replacement for Guigs. The British sales of *Morning Glory* had been reflected all over Europe and they were determined to concentrate on the worldwide success that seemed to be only a fingertip away. The future would always wait, but the 'now' was the only thing that mattered. Even without Guigs, they'd be able to prove something.

The first five gigs went really well, especially at Roseland in New York and the Orpheum in Boston, where the crowd seemed to really support a sound that defiantly offered an alternative to the increasingly lazy echoes of grunge. While they hadn't yet barged their way through the crack in the door, there was an affirmation that success was, at last, a conceivable option. In particular, the songs on *Morning Glory* had tugged an audience almost embarrassed to admit that they could appreciate the fact that, for the first time in thirty years, a British rock 'n' roll group had come up with a refreshingly coherent style that both accepted the security of the past and suggested something new, a loophole in the law that demanded blind worship of the likes of Pearl Jam or Hootie And The Blowfish.

In many ways Oasis had captured the only good elements of both those bands, but taken the displacement of the former and the commerciality of the latter, cranking up both, combining them and introducing a flourish that could never have existed in a world where aspirations always checked the possibility of heavy rotation on MTV. Oasis were singing stuff that came from the heart and, while it might have seemed quaintly odd in Britain, in America it was like torching the president. Saying in interviews with the American press that you don't much care about Stateside success is apparently tantamount to buggering your first born. When an audience start humming your tunes even after what you've said, you know you're on to something. A week in America had suggested just as much to the members of the band who'd been in America before.

Is the big 'but' going to mosey along? What do you think. Of course it is.

'We'd played this gig in Pittsburgh,' says Noel, 'and Scott went and sat on the bus afterwards with Margaret, our tour manager. The next day, she said, "He can't handle it, he's going home." He hadn't said anything to me or anyone else – he was just there one night and gone the next.'

Cutting short their tour and, yet again, cancelling their date in St Louis, the band made a cursory appearance on the *David Letterman Show* and flew back to Britain.

'Scott rung me when I'd got back,' says Noel. 'And he said, "Look, I think I made a mistake." I went, "Yeah, you made a big mistake. Bye." He let us down and he wasn't going to get a second chance.'

By now Guigs had grown tired of his self-enforced redundancy.

The recognition of boredom and a short course of Prozac had convinced him that there would never be a buzz like the feeling he got from playing with Oasis. He was back.

And back for the biggest gigs of Oasis's career. On 4 and 5 November they played Earls Court, the biggest indoor venue in Europe. Tickets sold out within hours, Oasis casually packing a place that it had taken David Bowie ten years to fill.

A week before the gig, an appearnace at La Luna in Brussels gave Guigs an almost desultory reintroduction to the rigmarole that he'd missed, but Earls Court was something else entirely.

A couple of weeks earlier I'd bumped into Noel at a Cast gig at London's Astoria. 'You've got to hear the guest list for Earls Court,' he'd said. 'Madonna, U2, Elton John, George Michael, McCartney, Pete Townshend, Oliver Reed, Stan Bowles, George Best, Ray Davies, Mick Jagger, Colin Bell, the lot. Everyone's either a genius or an alcoholic. Or both. It's going to be brilliant.'

And he was right.

Every pub within a couple of miles of Earls Court was packed to busting by lunchtime. And every jukebox was drowned out by communal karaoke renditions of all the songs that Oasis had ever recorded. Inside, the audience were just as voluble, politely applauding support act, the Bootleg Beatles, but saving their real enthusiasm for Oasis's extraordinary performances. The band had gone for a full-on extravaganza, complete with orchestra and, on the first night, enough volume to cause a mini-earthquake in the neighbourhood – enough to put most of the underground stations nearby out of action.

Earls Court is bigger than most countries. That became obvious as we were guided, on the first night, towards a backstage area easily as big as the 20,000-capacity space that we'd just left. Beyond the designated VIP area Pure Strings were reprising their instrumental version of *Morning Glory*, Oasis were celebrating in a Liechtenstein-sized backstage zone. By the Portakabin that constituted the 'official' dressing-room, you could, if you were lucky, get to touch the five neatly parked, pastel-coloured Italian scooters that Noel had bought the rest of the band as a celebratory present. Snooker player Alex 'Hurricane' Higgins, a regular attendee at Oasis gigs, was sitting in a corner telling anyone who'd listen that the band had a magic he'd only ever seen before with the Rolling Stones. Sid Cox, sans key fobs, graciously delineated a booster for the night ahead. Life was good.

'That Bono,' said Liam. 'We were having this conversation and he went, "I really like the stuff you're doing, son." I was, like, "Well, I think you've made some good records too, but I'm not your son."'

Maybe not linked by blood, but Oasis certainly seemed to be the natural successors to U2's brand of stadium-friendly rock and the Earls Court shows only emphasized the facility with which they handled their new status. And while it would have been easy to retreat into the pompous complacency that often defines that level of success, they managed to keep the same spark on giant stages that they'd possessed way back in half-empty back rooms of pubs. You got the feeling that it wasn't a case of them getting bigger, rather the world around them shrinking.

It was just as well, since they ended the year looking positively unstoppable. The last British show of the year was at Manchester's NYNEX Arena, and a sign of the regard in which Noel was held by fellow songwriters came when George Michael drove up with a dozen of his friends just to see the show. Noel himself still felt uncomfortable with the idea of a home-town performance and headed straight back to London immediately after the show. Liam, Robbie Williams and the actress Amanda Donahoe hosted an impromptu party in my room, the start of an epic drinking session that would result in Liam turning up late and much the worse for wear at the recording of the *Later With Jools Holland* TV show a couple of days later. At the first rehearsal, as the band unveiled their cover version of Slade's 'Cum On Feel The Noize', as well as orchestrally supplemented versions of 'Wonderwall' and 'Round Are Way', it soon became obvious that Liam's voice was shot to pieces. He stormed off stage and straight to the dressing-room to sleep, leaving Noel to do the singing for the actual performance. Afterwards the atmosphere understandably tense, everyone trooped home, in no mood for celebration.

It was time for the management to remind everyone that the partying had to calm down for a bit. A reminder that, come to think of it, they had been delivering since the day the band first went on stage. Now, however, there were real signs that all the hard work that had gone into cracking America was beginning to pay off. All those tours spent hawking the Oasis sound around towns all over America, including the Midwest (a place that aspirant British stars had hitherto treated merely as a stopover *en route* to LA or New York) had begun to pay dividends, building a fan base that had put the band at the top of the nation's college radio charts. *Definitely Maybe* had slowly but steadily built up sales of over half a million. The groundwork had been laid.

Oasis's music was always likely to be far more positively received by Americans than that of the likes of Suede or Blur, the most recent UK bands to be touted Stateside as contenders for superstar status. Whereas Brett Anderson and Damon Albarn's compositions drew on a uniquely British frame of reference, a whimsical, art-school foppery that had been as much of a handicap to David Bowie and the Kinks in the past, Oasis possessed a blue-collar directness that spoke as clearly to the psyche of the American heartland as the urban audience they had back home.

'They've got as much in common with Bruce Springsteen as with anyone else,' says Marcus Russell. 'They're rock 'n' roll songs by a rock 'n' roll band. It's as simple as that.'

And simplicity was to be the key. It came in the shape of 'Wonderwall'.

The first time Paul Weller heard 'Wonderwall' he proclaimed it the greatest song written so far in the nineties. And, in Britain, it remained in the higher reaches of the charts well into the new year, suggesting an ever-growing popularity with a whole new section of the public. It even got played on Radio 2.

In America it entered the *Billboard* charts at number twenty-one. In Britain the band had already enjoyed impressive-looking chart dominance (such as the week at the beginning of July '95 when six of their singles filled the top seven positions of the indie charts and five nestled in the 'proper' Top Seventy-five), but the sheer size of America, and the way that its charts depend as much on radio play as actual sales, made Oasis's success all the more impressive.

For thirty-one years the Beatles held the record for the highest-ever debut entry into the *Billboard* charts, coming in at number forty-five in 1964 with 'I Want To Hold Your Hand'. In October '95 Edwyn Collins's 'A Girl Like You' had entered at number forty-two. For Oasis to go in at twenty-one was a far greater achievement than was perhaps recognized even at the time.

The reason for the success of 'Wonderwall'? Basically because it sounded like the Beatles. Listeners were ringing radio stations asking to hear 'that Beatles song', genuinely convinced that it was an old song by the Fab Four, perhaps one of the numbers on the *Anthology* collection of rarities and out-takes. Even when they knew it was by Oasis they still kept on requesting it. The song touched something inside them, something that recalled the straightforward elegance of old songs by the Beatles and their contemporaries. Retro? Maybe. They didn't care. All the better for them than the disorientating vagaries of contemporary R&B or the dirty dregs of grunge. They listened to 'Wonderwall' and they understood.

Keep it simple. Remember. Keep it simple.

MTV backed 'Wonderwall' to the hilt, keeping the momentum

going for sales of the *Morning Glory* album, as did the radio release of the title track as a single. Some people have taken misguided delight in assuming that a record about cocaine abuse was being played all over an entire continent. In fact, as Noel told me the first time he played it, the lines 'All your dreams are made/When you're chained to the mirror and the razor blade' is all about having a shave in the morning. At least, that's all he's admitting.

By the time Oasis hit America late in the year for gigs in Seattle, Washington, Chicago, San Francisco, San Jose and LA, the album had already sold almost a million copies over there. By the time they left, sales were exceeding all expectations and, in the first week of 1996, having not pressed enough copies, Sony were left without a copy of the album to be had anywhere in the state of Florida.

Back in Britain, at the end of '95, Oasis could look back on one of the most extraordinary years in the history of British pop as a global power. As they prepared for an extended performance on Channel 4's *The White Room*, they were in understandably high spirits.

Sitting in a pub around the corner from the studios, Liam mixed easily with the fans. When they're in the mood, the band are only too happy to hang out with the people who've made them successful, and that was one of those days, Liam flirting playfully with the girls, politely rebuffing the earnest enquiries about B-sides from overawed young men and spending a couple of hours drinking for England.

He joked about the fun to be had from choosing ever more inventive aliases under which to check into hotels.

'We've got some good new ones,' he said. 'Ken Guru and Wally B are two of them. And Guigs has started using Mick Sgrill! They're getting weirder each time.'

Over in the dressing-room, Noel was in an equally good mood. Paul Weller had dropped by to say hello and the pair were reminiscing about the time the two of them last appeared on the show, doing a duet together. Bonehead came in with a Christmas card for everyone in the band, a disarmingly sweet gesture.

'I do it every year,' he said. 'They're my mates, aren't they?'

'Well, you're not getting one off me,' said Noel, coming over all Ebenezer Scrooge.

The performance itself was one of the best they've ever done for TV, Liam somehow managing not to appear to be sweating despite wrapping himself up in the sort of cagoule designed for Arctic survival.

Afterwards Creation hosted a Christmas party at the Halcyon Hotel in Holland Park, where they handed the band some very special Christmas presents. Drummer Alan White got a radio-controlled Mini Cooper (and the key to a real one), while for Bonehead there was a Rolex, for Liam a guitar and, for Guigs, membership of a gym. Nothing apparently for Noel.

'Come outside,' said Alan McGee, taking him out to the street.

'There's your present,' he said, pointing at a chocolate-brown Rolls-Royce Corniche parked outside.

For the first time in years Noel was lost for words.

'But I can't even drive,' he eventually managed.

Fortunately the car came with a chauffeur and a long-term reserved parking space in an underground car park, so he wouldn't have to leave such an ostentatious gift outside his house. McGee had recalled that when the band were starting and someone asked Noel what he wanted out of it all, he'd said he'd love a Rolls-Royce. Considering the turnover that Oasis had brought to Creation, it was the least he could do.

Liam was mouthily dismissive. 'All I get is a guitar and a fucking River Island shirt and he gets a car, the bastard.'

An understandable response, perhaps, but no one else present could begrudge Noel the Roller, especially after witnessing the gobsmacked delight with which he sat inside it and eagerly pressed all the knobs and switches to see what they did.

I sat in the front seat next to him and watched him try to come to terms with the most tangible reward yet of what he'd done with his life.

'This is fucking brilliant,' he said. 'It's bigger than my flat.'

Back at that flat a few weeks earlier, he'd first played me a tape of Mike Flowers's cabaret version of 'Wonderwall', enthusing about the interpretation. He also put on a Eurodisco version that his record company had sent to him for approval, fully expecting him to refuse to let it be released.

'I don't care what sort of cover versions people do as long as I get the royalties,' he reasoned. 'It's funny, so I'm all for it. Three years ago I gave you all that bullshit about how big we were going to be, and now we're sitting here with platinum discs all over the place listening to a load of Italians doing a disco version of one of my songs. Mad, isn't it?'

And the platinum discs were certainly piling up, filling all the wall space and stacked in corners.

'I went to Gracelands,' he said, 'and I saw this room that Elvis had that was like a tower about 200 feet high. It was covered in gold and platinum discs. The rate we're going, we're going to have that many by Christmas. They're going to have to start delivering them in lorries.'

Things were finally going well enough for them to relax for a bit. There'd even been something of a rapprochement with Blur at a recent MTV awards ceremony in Paris.

'I met Damon there,' said Liam. 'So I went in the dressing-room walking in slow motion and said, "Hellllooooo Daaaaamoooon, I'm from Maaaaanchesteeeeuur. We taaalk reeeally slooooooowly ooooop Noooorth 'cos weeeee're reeeeeally stuuuuupid. Have a good gig." It really freaked him out and they played shit. I went up to him afterwards and said, "You were shit." And he goes, "What do you mean, shit?" I'm going, "Well, just, like, shit. Your album's shit as well."

'So Damon goes, "Well, I think your album's shit," and I was, like, "Brilliant, let me buy you a drink. At last it's out in the open, let's be honest with each other." I don't mind the rivalry, but it's got to be out in the open. Graham out of Blur is a nice bloke, it's the rest of them that are cunts. I don't know why they don't stand up to their record company and come out and tell us they think we're shit. What are they scared of?'

Not that the awards ceremony went off without a hitch. At one point Liam tried to brain Michael Hutchence with a fire extinguisher after the latter started taking the piss out of him. And, back at the hotel, Brian Cannon managed to throw a chair out of his window, causing £1000 worth of damage. A rock 'n' roll gesture made all the more remarkable by the fact that he was in his room on his own at the time.

'It was the champagne,' he says by way of mitigation.

Noel had also managed to put the rivalry between Oasis and Blur into some sort of perspective.

'Of course it got on my nerves,' he told me. 'I was down the King's Road the day that Chelsea played Man United and I went into this pub. Someone put "Parklife" on the jukebox, like, nine times on the run. Can I cope? Of course I can fucking cope. I'm the one with the platinum discs and the money in the bank. I'm not exactly sobbing.'

And the Rolls-Royce. Don't forget the Rolls-Royce.

# 14

---

# BEST BRITS

Nineteen ninety-six started with both versions of 'Wonderwall' still in the charts and reflected success for a couple of Oasis tribute bands, the Gallaghers and No Way Sis. Both got the seal of approval from the real article, particularly the latter, whose gigs Noel regularly attends, 'cos it's like seeing us and I never get a chance to experience that.'

The band had also established a bond with the Bootleg Beatles, whose tribute act had provided the support at the Earls Court gigs. Better still, Noel had been hanging out with the real Paul McCartney, having been introduced both at the *Help* album recording session at Abbey Road and through a friendship with his daughter, Stella.

'I went round to his house,' says Noel, 'and he said, "You remind me a lot of what we were like, the whole look and everything." I said, "I should think so, I've spent enough money trying." Anyway, he'd heard *Morning Glory* and said he really liked some of the songs. It was a buzz to hear that.'

One rumour had it that McCartney said to Noel, 'You're going to run out of Beatles riffs to rip off before too long,' to which Noel replied, 'I don't think so, I've got all the bootlegs to get through yet.' Sadly, it turns out to be an apocryphal tale, but you won't find Noel too quick in denying it.

Besides, he'd already proved that Oasis were very much a match for anyone. In the British album charts they were being held off the top slot by the singing soldiers, Robson & Jerome, but were still higher placed than the Beatles, whose *Anthology* was at number three.

'If it hadn't been for Robson & Jerome, we'd have been number one and the Beatles number two,' says Noel. 'If that had happened I was going to take out a full-page ad with that bit of the chart blown up huge. Imagine us at number one, holding off the Beatles. That would have been the best moment of my life.'

In fact there was little time to muse over such indulgences, as *Morning Glory* had already taken up residency in the Top Five in the American album charts and was outselling all opposition in Europe. After a few dates in Germany, the band returned to Britain to play a short British tour, before announcing their biggest-ever dates, two shows at Maine Road in April. The 40,000 tickets for the first show sold out in under two hours, a similar amount for the second taking only another couple of hours to do the same. It was obvious that Oasismania was showing little sign of abating.

Not surprising then that a whole heap of awards continued to come their way. At the *NME* Brats ceremony, they picked up four – Best Album, Best Band, Best Single, and Best Live Act – and Noel even ended up with a couple of bizarre animal statuettes for the album from a Finnish magazine. They have pride of place on top of his TV set.

The big industry awards are the Brits, and it was no surprise to see them clean up at the ceremony, winning Best Band, Best Album and Best Video (for 'Wonderwall').

The band had spent much of the afternoon in the studio, and

Guigs confesses that they were enjoying themselves so much that they almost couldn't be bothered to turn up to the ceremony at Earls Court, the site of their earlier triumphant performances. When they eventually did turn up, they decided to go bonkers. There was a definite sense of vindication in that they trounced Blur in all categories, making up for the disappointment of losing out to them a year earlier. And, as the night drew on, they took full advantage of both drinking everything within arm's reach and publicly berating all opposition. Arguments ensued with host Chris Evans and again, backstage, with Michael Hutchence, a row that spilled over into the awards ceremony itself, Liam offering to accompany Hutchence outside for a scrap. In accepting their awards they found time, amid their defiantly obstreperous tomfoolery, to name-check Alan McGee and urge viewers to go out and vote Labour. Leader Tony Blair was there with his second-in-command, John Prescott, both of whom made an effort to acknowledge the band. After the awards, Prescott came up to the table where I was sitting with Guigs and said to the Oasis bassist, 'So, you're the main men I've heard about then?' No one was quite sure what on earth he was on about, but the fact that he recognized them was a source of some pleasure.

Michael Jackson's overblown, tastelessly Messianic performance at the awards had caused Jarvis Cocker from Pulp to embark on a one-man protest, invading the stage, wiggling his arse and flicking 'V' signs everywhere. His gesture was lost somewhat in the mêlée of Jackson's performance itself, but Cocker found himself hauled offstage and taken straight to the police station.

Later, back at the Landmark Hotel, where Oasis were celebrating their victory with another all-night partying session, Cocker turned up to a hero's welcome.

'It was brilliant what he did,' Noel enthused. 'He should have punched the fucker.'

Jarvis's behaviour took much of the post-Brits tabloid attention away from Oasis, and most of their comments were cut from the orginally broadcast version of the show (although they were restored for an uncut late-night version that went out several weeks later).

'I really don't care what people think about how we behaved at the Brits,' Noel maintains. 'It was full of all these record industry dicks who'd told us how we were never going to make it, and we were just rubbing their noses in it a bit. You can't go to something like that and play along with the stupid game where you're supposed to slap everyone else on the back and tell them how brilliant you think they are. The organizers had asked us to play at the Brits a year earlier, and when we refused they said, "Well, you'll never win anything anyway." Then there we were this year getting every fucking award going. And we'll never get invited back again, which has to be a good thing.'

Meanwhile the band were celebrating their second number one with the single release of 'Don't Look Back In Anger'. They had filmed a video for it at *Avengers* star Patrick McNee's mansion in America on their last visit, but weren't particularly pleased with the finished version, complete with dancing girls and an awkward flippancy.

The sleeve of the single, however, was their most lavish to date, costing more than anything before it, including the covers of the two albums.

To promote the single on *Top Of The Pops*, they were invited on to do two songs, a privilege given to only a handful of acts in the show's history. And, despite some brazenly bored miming at the piano from Liam, their performance was genuinely thrilling as they ended 'Don't Look Back In Anger' and rammed into their cover of 'Cum On Feel The Noize' via an onstage pyrotechnic explosion that virtually levelled the studio.

In unstoppable mood, they headed back to America for a series of East Coast dates that saw them more enthusiastically received than ever before. Ben Stud of *Melody Maker* travelled out to see them in Philadelphia and found that, while some of the newspaper critics were less than enamoured by what they saw as a dull retread of the Beatles, the fans themselves saw in Oasis a genuinely new future for the American rock environment. Admittedly, the fans' theories often came out as merely 'neat' or 'cool', but, as an instinctive response, it blew away all doubts about whether the stranglehold of grunge could be broken.

Ben Stud was equally impressed. 'The greatest rock 'n' roll band in the world?' he asked at the end of his piece, immediately answering his own question: 'I have not a single doubt.'

Ben's *Melody Maker* interview with Noel included a quote from the latter about how the band were 'lads' and how their upbringing and background were always going to affect what they did and how they behaved.

'We've burgled houses and nicked car stereos and we like girls and we swear and take the piss,' said Noel, making a point with dramatic effect rather than seriously confessing to a life of crime.

Nevertheless, reports of his quote resulted in Manchester's police reopening several lines of enquiry into unsolved burglaries in an unbelievably naïve or incredibly stupid attempt to hold the band responsible for the city's entire crime figures for the past five years. There were the usual rent-a-quote outbursts from campaigners for 'family' values, people who failed to appreciate that this particular family were bringing more into the country's coffers by way of taxable income than most major industrial conglomerates. Instead of calling for their immediate incarceration, you'd think they'd be nominating them for positions on the board of directors. Noel, after all, who once worked for British Gas, was now earning more than the chairman.

Not that the band were particularly concerned at the furore. When Liam was asked by a *Daily Mirror* reporter whether there was any truth to the accusations of burglary, he deadpanned, 'Yeah, I've done loads. I'm doing your house tonight.'

A week after the Philadelphia gig I went to see them in New York for the closing date of the tour. The level of their success was made all the more obvious by the opulence of the band's hotel, the Rihga Royal on Manhattan's Upper West Side, less than a block from the TV studio where the Beatles played when they first came to America. The Rihga Royal is an all-suite hotel, much plusher than the usual rock 'n' roll hang-outs favoured by visiting musicians. A serious-money place. Oh, and there's a tiny, neighbourhood Irish bar around the corner where you can stay up all night drinking Guinness. The night before, that's exactly what Oasis had done, but the evening I arrived they, their crew and old buddy Robbie Williams were back for more of the same.

A spectacularly drunk Robbie was as entertaining as ever, going up to a tramp and giving him a hundred dollars because 'he looked a bit hungry', before realizing that the man wasn't a tramp at all, just someone walking by. It was not the wisest of benevolent gestures, particularly since he was left with only forty cents himself, but as good an excuse as any for drinking a whole lot more.

Patsy Kensit had also flown over to surprise Liam, and while his initial reaction had suggested that he didn't much like surprises, the two had retired to a corner to talk. Everyone else trooped back to the hotel to empty the bar, defiantly unconcerned about the show the next day.

It was a landmark gig. Held at the Paramount, an annex of Madison Square Garden, it had sold out in a matter of hours. The only person who seemed to be nervous was Richard Ashcroft, singer with the recently disbanded the Verve, who had been invited by Oasis to play his first solo performance.

He needn't have worried. Such was the buzz among the audience that they weren't about to give anyone a hard time, and it did no harm that Ashcroft's new songs were sparkling examples of genius songwriting. Noel had written about Ashcroft in the Oasis song, 'Cast No Shadow', addressing the complexities in the mind of one of rock's most consistently underrated songsmiths. That night in New York, he more than convinced the crowd of his abilities.

Oasis went down a storm. Despite the fact that it was far from being one of their best performances, they could afford to cruise through the proceedings, getting by merely on the strength of their songs and the tornado at their heart that can blow the roof off buildings even when whirling on half strength. A crowd unused to such economic dynamism were left reeling with delight.

Downstairs in the dressing-room the record company had plastered the walls with Union Jacks and left similarly embossed key fobs all over the place, presumably having only just heard of Britpop, and managed to get the wrong end of the stick completely. The band did their best to ignore them, concentrating instead on acknowledging superstar visitors like Johnny Depp and John McEnroe, both of whom seemed to turn up at every NY Oasis gig.

The post-gig party moved back to the Irish bar, where old face Evan Dando turned up, along with Lars from Metallica, singularly a hard-core Oasis fan. Much of the rock 'n' roll behaviour had already taken place before the gig, when Liam smashed in his TV set because he was 'sick of going up and down in lifts all the time'. Not an explanation that the hotel manager, or indeed anyone else in the world, found particularly enlightening.

Back in my room, Liam complained about the downside of American success.

'We're big here, so we shouldn't have to do all the shit still, but we have to do more interviews than ever with stupid photographers pushing you around like you're a piece of furniture or something. I like the fans getting into it all, but everyone else can fuck off. I've had enough of them. You don't get any time to do anything. I'll be glad to get back home.'

Another reason for his displeasure was the hint that there might be some truth behind the rumours that the FBI were keeping a dangerously close eye on the band, ready to deport them as soon as the opportunity arose. That afternoon, Liam had bought a new pair of jeans and left them in a locked dressing-room. When he got back someone had planted three wraps of cocaine in the back pocket. To his credit he threw them away immediately, but it was clear that the incident had shaken him. Things were getting a bit wobbly, and it was fortunate that the band were flying back to Britain the next morning.

Again Liam emphasized how he'd like to write some songs, quoting lyrics from one that he was halfway through writing. It was called 'Mirrory Puddles' and was, as far as I can recall, a little too, er, left-field to fit snugly into the Oasis scheme of things, but he repeated his desire to play a more creative role.

'I'm going to write a classic. It might be tomorrow or it might be in ten years' time, but I'm going to do it. Just wait.'

As the night rolled on, fuelled by rather more than cups of strong coffee, he spiralled into a hundred different rants, but whereas a while back they could easily have turned into something with serious ramifications for the future of the group, this time they seemed more like just a way of unfurling all the little irritations that inevitably accompany the ritual of touring. He was pissed off, but it wouldn't matter in the morning. There was the future to think of.

Suddenly it *was* morning, and the most immediate bit of that future involved remembering what room he was staying in, finding his clothes, packing and getting down in another of those lifts to the hotel lobby, outside which the tour coach was already waiting with its engine running. Oasis and early-morning flights will, one suspects, never be terrifically well suited.

The next months saw the band touring Europe, playing gigs in Dublin and Cardiff and returning to America for a final Stateside flourish. They knew it was time to wind down somewhat, aware that much of the latter part of the year would be spent on the road. And, as *Morning Glory* continued to sell by the lorry-load, Marcus was keen to ensure that their progress could be kept under control. While it would have been easy to keep on putting out singles off the album, particularly in America (where there had been talk of releasing 'Champagne Supernova'), it was decided to take the foot off the accelerator for a bit and wait until the beginning of '97 before bringing any more records out.

'It gives people a chance to miss us,' says Liam.

There would be time for a break, but first there were their two biggest gigs to date to get out of the way. Maine Road, a return to their field of dreams.

Noel went to see Pink Floyd play at Maine Road once, on account of his love of the album *The Wall*. And, of course, he and his brother used to go there every fortnight to see City play. In late '94 he'd even played football there as part of a half-time guest appearance for Sky TV. He'd whacked a ball at the goal at the Kippax End, a screamer from the edge of the box. It had hit the post.

'There were thousands of people shouting, "You're shit" at me,' he says. 'It was more nerve-racking than any gig.'

Liam was there too that day, knocking his shot in from a couple of yards. And hurting his foot in the process.

'The ball bobbled,' explained Liam.

'It was weird being allowed to run on the pitch without being thrown off,' recalls Noel.

By the time of the Maine Road gigs, Oasis had a long-established friendship with the City staff and many of the players (who come along to their shows). When 'Some Might Say' went to number one, they got a congratulatory telegram from City's Francis Lee, and one of their earliest investments was their own executive box at the ground. Sales of Manchester City merchandise rocketed in direct proportion to the band's success.

Before the Manchester NYNEX Arena show, Manchester United player Ryan Giggs had rung up Oasis's office, trying to get on the guest list along with some of his team-mates. Liam told him to fuck off. In the week before the Maine Road gigs, he met the United player again in a nightclub and relentlessly took the piss out of him, accusing him of, among other things, 'just being able to run fast'. But the band did agree to put the United team on the list for the gigs, their names joining a couple of hundred other footballers, musicians and TV personalities. That weekend, they were the biggest pull in the country.

The two shows were extraordinary, but the practicalities of organizing anything on such a large scale inevitably produced problems. The band had registered bookings at almost every hotel in Manchester to throw fans off the scent, but the roads around the stadium were so jammed that they had to spend most of each day inside the venue itself. Also, an almost non-existent security presence outside the ground meant a field day for the local urchins of Moss Side, most of whom seemed to spend the entire forty-eight hours in surrounding streets stealing tickets and trying to sell them on for as much as £300 each. In the quiet moments in between, they whiled away the time throwing stones at anyone passing by. Hardly surprising for an area as notoriously dangerous as it was, but it led to a lot of nasty scenes that could easily have spilled over into a full-scale riot.

'I'm a socialist,' says Alan McGee, 'but it tested even my faith in people. You look at places like that, though, and you see that crime is one of the only ways out.'

Another is pop music. And, in many ways, Oasis are an iconic alternative to those very people with the Stanley knives and their own twist on the entrepreneurial impulse. The lads. One of them even blagged his way into the hospitality area, white cagoule zipped to the neck, moving with the familiar Liam lope. And 40,000 heads turned in the stadium, thinking it was him, cheering and waving. For a moment he *was* Liam. It's the dream at the heart of Oasis's appeal.

For two nights on stage, Oasis showed just how intoxicatingly majestic that dream can be. Playing better than ever before and holding an aggregate audience of 80,000 people in the palm of their hand. It was one of the most emotionally powerful moments of my life. And, when they got round to thinking about it all, the band generally agreed they were the finest gigs they've ever done. Both nights were filmed and taped for an as yet unspecified commercial release sometime in the future.

After the triumph, a chance to relax for the first time in three years. The band went home to girlfriends, bought houses, chilled out. Noel and Meg moved out of Camden and into a large house in St John's Wood, while Liam moved in with Patsy in preparation for buying a place of his own. He'd already been close to buying a place in Stockport, having been given details of a hundred different properties by an estate agent, and plumped simply for the first one that came to hand. 'It's opposite a girls' school,' he had reasoned sensibly.

While they weren't actually making any records, their profile became, if anything, higher than ever. Puppet models of them on *Spitting Image* and paparazzi shots of them in almost every day's papers only served to emphasize how firmly they have become lodged in the cultural consciousness.

Not that Noel in particular was exactly hiding from the cameras. The man who admits that he'll go to any gig that's on, so low is his boredom threshold, also took advantage of the flurry of party invites that were thrown his way, even being asked his professional opinion on *Mission: Impossible* at the film's première.

He did get to fulfil another enduring ambition at the Royal Festival Hall when he sang onstage with his hero Burt Bacharach, his rendition of 'This Guy's In Love With You' well received by an audience that included Liam.

'I was more scared doing that than anything I've ever done before,' says Noel, whose dedication to Bacharach is so obsessive that he even possesses a programme for one of the man's seventies shows, and takes great delight in revealing that Burt had a pet duck called Quack Quackarach.

Just to show that Oasis really do have the Midas touch, the band allowed a German TV station to use 'Don't Look Back In Anger' as the nation's official theme for coverage of the Euro '96 football tournament. Germany, inevitably, won.

When you're the biggest band in the world, you're not supposed to take it easy. Stepping back to appreciate everything you've achieved becomes an open invite to all the dumb scavengers, the dickheads who huff and puff and finally get within hailing distance of the opportunity to make a quick buck. As Oasis took a breather, their sky was clogged with brainless vultures. One company paid for Noel and Meg to go to the Cannes Film Festival, hiring a private jet for them, putting them up in the best hotel rooms, the whole VIP treatment. All to try and wrench a lucrative publishing deal out of someone they'd smugly ignored when they had the chance to back him years earlier. He took the bait, lived it up, had a good time – and told them no.

Sony were just as eager to take advantage of a guaranteed money-earner. They tried to buy out Alan McGee's crucial two percent of Creation's controlling interest, something which would tug ultimate control away from the man who understands exactly why Oasis mean much more than just a vehicle for churning out profits.

'I've got an obsessive personality,' says McGee, 'and I remember one day I was in this shop buying loads of lottery tickets. Noel came in and he went, "What the fuck are you doing?" I said, "Well, you never know, I might win." He said, "Why do you need the lottery?

You've got us." And he was right. They mean more to me than just money, though. I still get excited when I hear a new song. Anyone who doesn't love them and have total belief in them doesn't deserve to be involved with anything they do. I was at this big meeting with Sony and I told them, "Well, if you want the label, then Oasis and the Primals and everyone else are going to leave." It was like a great big poker game. They got the message in the end, and we just renewed the old deal for five years. And I walked out with a banker's draft for fourteen and a half million quid. You can't try and turn Oasis into some sort of marketing thing. They're more important than that.'

Three months off, and the band now prepared to prove it to themselves as much as to the people around them. The snapshots and the memories were all very well, but adoration is a hard habit to kick. They weren't about to drift away from the allure of mass appreciation. They had to get back to playing live. Just like breathing, but bigger.

# 15

---

# BUZZING FOR TOMORROW

Late July, and London's week-long heat wave turns to oppressive humidity and vicious thunderstorms. The sky's guts split apart to a background of whiplash cracks and pyrotechnic lightning. Rivers of rain threaten to make a moat of the car park surrounding the equatly anonymous South London industrial estate.

It's a grim place at the best of times. Less than a mile from the City's old heart, the Tower of London, these days little more than an Olde Worlde theme park for tourists, the estate is typical of the post-war degeneration that has carved up most of the capital south of the Thames. Concrete jungle tower blocks patrolled by the psychotically disaffected, the twitchily suspicious and others that have simply given up caring. If you're not glassy-eyed, you're marked out immediately as not from around these parts. Random acts of violence tend to do for introductions.

Those areas that are not defined – somewhat optimistically – as habitable, are taken up by barbed-wire fortresses of free enterprise. Lorries rumble in and out, collecting and depositing at generic warehouses identified only by apparently arbitrary sets of initials. There are few clues as to what goes on in these places, and even less of an impression that anyone wants you to find out. Let your imagination run riot and you can envisage any activity you like, any side of legality.

The reality is much more likely to be drearily commonplace. A local subcentre for the distribution of pallets, or small-scale machine part manufacture, perhaps. The mundane tick-tock of just making a living.

You might expect a lot of things as you drive past in the pouring rain. Everything except the most popular rock 'n' roll band in the Western world giving it big time.

But that's just what's happening.

Music Bank belies the inauspicious name-plate that shares space on a steel door with another of those jumbled-up series of initials. Inside and up two flights of stairs, however, you can tell you're in one of those record industry enclaves where money's not exactly a stranger. Soundproof sliding windows, heavy pine doors and tasteful wall-to-wall carpeting give the undeniably confident impression of a place where the winners end up. Where financial security can buy a well-appointed cocoon.

Three years from that damp, gloomy rehearsal room under the Manchester Boardwalk to this. For Oasis, the past is not just another country – it's a whole different planet.

Between Maine Road and now they've had their longest holiday, their only holiday, since they first started. A time to actually appreciate the rewards that their success has brought and to relax into the 'real' life that'll be there for them for ever more. A time for chilling out, hanging with wives and girlfriends, wallowing in the luxury of waking up with a hangover and not having to head straight off to a sound check. The payback.

Still, the lure of work has been hard to kick, and even though it's only been three months you can sense that they've begun to get bored with all that time on their hands. They're hungry again for the buzz from the crowd that they'd almost taken for granted, ready to reclaim the spotlight.

And so, ten days before the two Loch Lomond gigs that will be immediately followed by performances in Stockholm, Knebworth, Cork and . . . everywhere, they regroup for a confidence-reasserting rehearsal. In three days they'll go up to Birmingham's NEC to do a proper run-through on a stadium-sized stage, teaming up with ex-Stone Roses guitarist John Squire, who has been asked to guest on a couple of their songs when they play live. Today, though, they're just limbering up, readjusting to life back in the bubble.

And from the first, it's just like they never went away.

You can hear them from down the corridor. The familiar unfurling guitar lines from 'Some Might Say', Liam's voice trampolining off the walls with an elasticity that curiously recalls the times when he still had something to prove, when he couldn't just walk onstage and busk it. There's muddiness to the sound, but it's due more to the smallness of the room than any ring-rustiness. You can't ignore the ebullience. They're back.

Behind the curtained-off entrance, there's a wide, low stage, one of the monitors emblazoned with a large Manchester City logo. In front of the stage there's a camera tracking along specially installed rails, and all around them are a gaggle of people shooting video, Super Eight and the odd snapshot. Brian Cannon is making a documentary, a project born out of the fact that he's been asked to make a three-minute short that will be projected on a giant screen during the 'Swamp Song' instrumental that will start the forthcoming live shows.

'I'm not doing a documentary for the money,' says Cannon. 'I'm just going to shoot film of them during the next year. When they're recording the album, at some of the shows, wherever. It's stuff that has to be documented 'cos in the future it's going to be important. You look back on all that old Beatles footage and you think, I'm glad someone had a camera filming all that. That's what all this is for. We've already got seven hours on film and there's going to be loads more. If it was done by some outsider, it would end up really fake, but this is just hanging around with them and they know it's people they trust. It's family.'

I'm there to ask some questions, get them to tell the archives what they're all about these days, give them somewhere to lob the cockiness. On this occasion chirpy camaraderie is just about the last thing I feel like initiating, having found out a couple of hours earlier that my friend Rob Collins (keyboardist with the Charlatans, who were due to support Oasis at Loch Lomond and Knebworth) had died in a car crash the previous night. But as soon as eye contact is made, it's obvious that at least I won't have to endure any tiresome petulance. Everyone in the band is in good shape and seemingly rejuvenated by the time off.

They're tanned, comfortable and dressed with that slightly scruffy casualness that only the seriously rich can ever really pull off. As Liam stands behind the mic in baggy shorts, arms behind his back and mouth singing to the ceiling, the iconic pose that's instantly identifiable, I find myself wondering what it is about him that seems to come from somewhere so long ago. Then I realize. He's smiling. He's really enjoying it.

And so is Noel. Shirt untucked, he's hammering away at a Union Jack guitar, every inch the end-of-the-century Mod God. He swaps jokes with Guigs, Bonehead and Alan, all looking like they've remembered why being in a band always seemed so good in the first place.

And when one of the sound crew inadvertently loosens a lead, filling the room with feedback, there's no tetchy vindictiveness, just a genial joshing about how it would all be a lot simpler if everyone fucked off with the twiddling about and just let them get on with it. It's an atmosphere that's been away for a long, long time.

Oasis run through most of the set they intend playing at the forthcoming shows, restoring 'Columbia' to the top of the proceedings and including all the singles bar 'Shakermaker'. 'Masterplan' and 'Round Are Way', the B-sides that went down so well at Maine Road, are also given a place in the first team. Towards the end, they give the first live performances of two new songs, 'My Big Mouth' and 'Gettin' Better, Man', both of which bode well for the third album.

Footballs get kicked about, the cameras keep on rolling, and the smallest gig they've done, or will do, for years, ends in unqualified approval from the dozen-strong audience.

Afterwards there are brief exchanges of condolences about Collins's death, but so close to the time when Oasis are to leap back on to the carousel, it's understandably not something anyone wants to talk about too much. Intimations of mortality can't be allowed to intrude on the optimism. It wouldn't be fair to anybody.

Liam goes outside into the sunshine after the rain. The rehearsal space looks out over the whole of London, and it's weird to think that in every room of every building as far as you can see, there are people who have heard of Oasis. Maybe not people who like them, or even care about them, but people who've heard all the same. It's a slightly unnerving thought. And when Liam waves at the passengers in a train dawdling by and someone jokes that they'll probably all pull the communication cord and jump out, the possibility doesn't seem entirely remote.

'I've just been in Capri,' says Liam, 'and people used to just come up and shout, "Autograph". With Patsy they'd come up and talk to her and tell her how beautiful she was. With me it was just, "Sign this". I was like, wait a minute, what about all the "You're so great" stuff?' In the past he would genuinely have been bothered. Nowadays he's grown up, can actually appreciate the daftness of the situation and of his role in other people's fantasy. He's comfortable with it.

Not that he hasn't got a few fantasies of his own.

'We went on this yellow submarine,' he enthuses. 'It was brilliant. It wasn't like a huge thing, just a few people. And you go down and see all these mad starfish and things. I was just sitting there going, "We all live in a yellow submarine, a yellow submarine . . ." It'd be great to do a video on it.'

As with the rest of the band, it was his first break in ages and, while he enjoyed it, he's keen to play live again.

'I'm right up for these gigs,' he says. 'I've been chilling out, taking it easy, but now I'm ready to go mad again. The gigs are going to be great.'

Do you like the celebrity?

'It's just a job. It's something that I need to do for me, though. I mean, you can have fun doing anything. You could have fun driving that train. It's just something I do, man. And when I'm doing it, I don't remember much about it. I can't remember anything about Maine Road. I remember watching *Antiques Roadshow* before we went on, but that's it. All I know is, I'm mad for doing these gigs and doing the album and everything. I want to get back into it all again.'

In the meantime he's got some more of the trappings afforded by his fame and success to sort out. Namely putting an offer in on a gorgeous house by a river in Hertfordshire that he's got his eye on. Six bedrooms, snooker room, adjoining cottage and acres ahoy. A nice place to keep the expensive car he bought a few months ago off a car dealer called, really, Mr Crook.

'Yeah,' he jokes. 'I gave him twenty grand in cash, went round the corner and it fell to pieces.' He keeps the guy's business card in his pocket, aware of the delicious flourish that it gives the fuck-off gesture of buying such a car in the first place.

Are you happy, Liam?

'Of course I'm happy. What do you think?'

It had to be asked. Just for the hell of it.

As the sky darkens, and the monsoon rolls back over, we adjourn inside to the ante-room to hear a rough tape of the next Oasis album, working title: *Be Here Now*.

It's good. Very good. And it's going to blow away any premature declarations that Oasis have peaked.

'I always wanted to do the third album,' says Liam. '*Morning Glory* was all right, but I knew we could do better. And this next one is going to prove it.'

The rough tape starts with a trippy guitar instrumental, out of which suddenly roars the sound of a jetliner landing. It's a searing, defiantly rock opening, building a sound that's picked up by all the songs that follow. Numbers like the aforementioned 'My Big Mouth' and 'Gettin' Better, Man' have lodged into the subconscious after only a couple of listens, but the rest of the stuff is just as good. Titles like 'Fade In/Out', 'Stand By Me', 'All Around The World' (that particular one written almost three years ago) and 'Girl In The Dirty Shirt' all suggest that when the album is released in 1997, it should emphasize that it's far too early to even think about writing the band off.

'I want to get that "Strawberry Fields" feel,' says Noel, 'and a different feel to *Morning Glory*. If the first album was a soundtrack for going out on the piss and the second was for staying at home having a shag, then the next one's going to be about staying at home having a shag and going straight back out on the piss again afterwards.'

A couple of years ago, after almost every Gallagher brothers interview degenerated into argumentative chaos, Noel and Liam decided not to do any more interviews together. Any points that they'd wanted to put across always seemed to have been over-shadowed by the vicariously easy squabbling siblings stories. And didn't do much for the state of mind of either of them.

Today, however, in their freshly positive mood and surrounded by people they know they can trust, they've got no qualms about sitting side by side on the sofa and talking about their immediate future and their recent past. They'll playfully take the piss out of each other, but never even come close to the kind of antagonism that marked so many of their early dual encounters with journalists.

So, what have they been up to?

'Just taking it easy,' says Noel. 'Going out, going on holiday, getting fat.'

Both of them reveal their stomachs, each able to pinch a good deal more than an inch.

'That's what success gets you,' says Noel. 'A really big stomach. Oh yeah, and I've been making lots of money too.'

A few days earlier, he'd been up in Wales remixing the new single by American loopy post-folk performer, Beck.

'Do you know how much I got for that Beck thing?' he asks, turning to whisper pantomimically in Liam's ear.

'Is that in pounds?' asks Liam.

'No, Venezuelan escudos. Loads of money. It's great.'

Not that he'd ever have been happy to stop working completely. Even a recent holiday in Mustique with girlfriend Meg and celeb friends, the actor Johnny Depp and model Kate Moss, couldn't drag him away from his guitar. I'd heard that he'd finally got over his dislike of dancing, having to be dragged off tables at the end of each night, but it seems that he hadn't entirely forgotten his *raison d'être*.

'I wrote loads of the stuff for the next album,' he says. 'And Owen and I demo'd it over there. Now we're right up for doing these gigs.'

Any memories of Maine Road?

'The gigs themselves were brilliant, probably the best we've ever done, and the bits where we were on stage were great. It was just all the shit around it that I hated. Getting the coach to and from the gig and all the gangs outside. That was just a hassle, but I really enjoyed the shows.'

'The first night was the best,' says Liam.

'Nah, the second was better,' Noel counters.

'That was good, but it rained,' concludes Liam.

No arguments, no fist-fights. Grown up at last. Both of them.

With all the organizational hassles, why play such large shows in the first place?

'Everything's got so big, that it's the only thing we can do,' says Noel. 'I mean, there's a quarter of a million people who want tickets, and the only way they're going to get them is if we do something like Loch Lomond or Knebworth. And if you make a big event out of it, it becomes really special. They're going to be good gigs.'

As good as those ones a couple of years back in front of a hundred people?

'Even better. I say that, but to be honest, I can't remember a lot of those old gigs like the 100 Club. I've seen photos and it looked like we were brilliant, but if I try to remember it, I can't. It's just a blank. I'd like to play there again, actually. Maybe we should do a secret tour of lost or little places. Like Earls Court!'

'Or,' he continues, warming to the idea, 'how about Manchester Boardwalk? Yeah, a 550-night residency at the Boardwalk. That's what we should do.'

Anywhere else?

'I'd still like to play Wembley Stadium . . .'

Liam splutters. 'What! Wembley Stadium is shit. We're not playing there.'

'It'd be a laugh,' insists Noel. 'Everyone ought to do it once.'

'Well, you can fucking do it on your own,' Liam rightly decides. 'There's no way I'm going to play there. It's a dump.'

Before they get round to arguing that one to a bloody and bruised conclusion, they're going to have to fulfil the contractual obligations that will find them on tour for much of the rest of the year. They've already arranged gigs in Sweden, France, America, Japan and Hong Kong, as well as a long-awaited trip to Australia, where they are easily the most popular band in the country. The Aussies even drew up a petition with several hundred thousand names demanding that Oasis make the twenty-four-hour flight over to play to them.

Their manager, Marcus Russell, comes in, constantly interrupted by calls on his mobile phone. He looks as healthy and relaxed as the rest of them. Obviously the rest has done everyone in their entourage a lot of good.

And given the tabloids the chance to come up with some spectacularly imaginative rumours. In the *Sunday Mirror* a few days earlier there'd been a story about Marcus's intent to buy a rugby club with the money he's made from Oasis.

'I've got a lot of things I could do with my money,' admits Russell, 'but buying a rugby club isn't one of them. Can you imagine what a crap thing that would be to do?'

He tells the band about a gig they've been booked to do in Hawaii. 'Just a small one: two and a half thousand people.' But Hawaii all the same.

It's a poetically neat location to blur the line between work and play, since it was in Hawaii that Alan McGee first heard a tape of 'Live Forever' and decided that he had a world-shaking band on his hands. And it also fulfils a promise that Marcus made to the band when he first tried to convince them to have him as their manager.

Noel adopts a cod-Welsh accent as he recalls how Marcus sat them down and said, 'Sign with me, boys, and you'll be playing Hawaii in two and a half years. I promise you.'

'He was right,' Noel admits, 'but it took three years, not two and a half. So we'll go over and play the gig, then we'll sack him. Hawaii's going to be good, though. It's full of chicks, isn't it? And we can bury Bonehead in the sand so just his head's showing, then people will come along, think he's a coconut and bash his head in. Oh yeah, I'm looking forward to going there.'

Any more ambitions?

'Musical or personal?'

Either.

'Personally, I'd really like to . . . no I can't say that.'

And he swerves from revealing something that it's safe to assume would be gushy, heartfelt and involving Meg.

'I can tell you what I'd like to do. I'd like to commit serious bodily harm on someone. And they know who they are.'

A lot more like the expected public face of Oasis.

Anything less, er, enigmatic?

'I'd like to learn to drive. Get some more money. Write some more songs, make some more records. Just keep on doing what we've been doing.'

Liam?

'Dunno, I'm up for everything at the moment. I want to play some gigs again, buy a house, do the next album, whatever. I wouldn't mind doing some films. Or some collaborations. That'd be good.'

Would you make a good actor?

'I'd be a good painter and decorator. Yeah, Batman or some-thing. I'd be well up for that.'

'We don't make plans so far ahead any more,' says Noel. 'In the beginning we had to because we were focusing on what we wanted. Now we can afford to do what we want. Who knows what we'll be doing in two years? Probably sitting here with you again, telling you how much things have changed since Knebworth.'

'Yeah,' says Liam. 'We'll be telling you how much we're looking forward to playing Buckingham Palace Gardens or somewhere like that.'

Any messages for the fans coming along to your gigs?

'Stand in front of my side of the stage 'cos I'm the best-looking one,' says Noel.

'No way,' interjects Liam. 'Stand at my side of the stage. I'm much better-looking than him.'

Noel spots a technicality. 'You haven't got a side of the stage, you dick. You're in the middle, remember?'

'OK, well, stand in front of my middle then.'

'I dunno about any messages,' says Noel. 'Come along, have a good time, clap at the end of the songs, just do what you do at gigs.'

'And,' warns Liam, 'if you see Brian Cannon, just go up and stare at him. Whisper, "Microdot, Microdot, Microdot" and freak him out.'

Everything comes so easy these days. Does that make it harder to come up with records that are actually going to touch anybody?

'It's all about the songs,' says Noel. 'People are only going to keep going out to buy your records if you've got the songs to back it all up. And we have. There's fifteen done for the next album, but I've got loads more ready to go right now. Maybe I shouldn't be saying that in case the song publishing people are interested. So, no, I haven't got any songs at all except for the ones on the album. Not one. I do know, though, that this band has always been about having great songs and we always will. We're not going to get lazy and just put out a load of shit. Everything we do takes things another stage further than they were before.'

And with that they're up and gone – Liam off to see Patsy, Noel off to Camden to buy a Lambretta, scooters having become almost as enticing a drain on his disposable income as guitars. He's even talked about getting special scooter flight cases made so the band can take them on tour with them.

They've all the trappings of the archetypal rich pop stars, and many groups before them have marked that as exactly the point where things came unglued, security robbing them of the solidarity and drive that defined their rise to prominence. The moment when your sound gets as flabby as your stomach.

I may be completely wrong, but I've an idea Oasis aren't going to fade away quite so easily. The tapes of the next album certainly suggest that it's far too early to start talking of their career being over. And, having overcome so many calamities, there's a feeling that they're actually enjoying the creativity that can come from not having to wake up nursing as many grudges and bruises as sore heads. They could be just about to embark on their most artistically worthwhile work to date. And then there's still a whole universe of possibilities.

When they first got together there were loads of people ready to tell them they'd never make it. And when they started to sell, almost as many smugly warned about how they'd never make it in America. Now that they have broken down the industry's defences Stateside, the soothsayers of doom are resolutely insisting that no one is ever truly going to match the status of the Beatles or the Stones. This despite the fact that a recent poll established them as more popular than the Beatles among under-twenty-fives in Britain, while year-end record sales confirmed them as the best-selling rock band on the planet.

Oasis are already arguably one of the ten most important rock bands in musical history, and it's clear that there's still a whole lot more to come.

On a personal level they've given me more pleasure and inspiration than any other group, as people as much as artists. And I'm sure there are an awful lot of others whose life they've changed. It's been a wild three years, and I feel genuinely privileged to have been so close to it all. I still tingle every time I see them play live, and I can't imagine a time when their records won't affect me as powerfully as they do. But I'm just as captivated by the possibilities their future still holds as by the worth of what they've already done. Oasis, I thank you.

And I'm buzzing for tomorrow.

# POSTSCRIPT

And then . . .

Well, the picnic got napalmed.

As even a passing acquaintance with the Oasis impulse has already relentlessly demonstrated, life's intricate machinery is gagging to be dismantled and scattered across the kitchen floor. Their innate talent has continually insisted on an all-back-to-mine for Old Ma Chaos and the Cataclysm Clan. Their success was always almost incomprehensibly swiftly attained and, while no one was about to disregard the thrall in which they were held by so many fans by Summer '96, it was retrospectively obvious that something had to give.

Pear shaped? Again? 'Fraid so.

Liam Gallagher sits on a sofa in San Francisco's plush Pan Pacific Hotel in June 1997.

'It's been a weird fucking year,' he says.

And it all started so well.

On 4 and 5 August 1996, Oasis played two stunning gigs at a breathtakingly picturesque site next to Loch Lomond in Scotland. Tickets for the Knebworth gigs sold out within four hours and promoters MCP say that the Knebworth and Loch Lomond performances were the fastest selling shows in the UK ever, five per cent of the country's population ringing up to get tickets.

The Loch Lomond shows, particularly the second night, will go down as among the best the band have ever played, their long-time dedicated Scottish fan base once again proving they know exactly how to corral Oasis' hedonistic intentions.

Back at Glasgow's Hilton Hotel they hosted a select soiree in a back room. Patsy proudly showed me her engagement ring, while Liam came to terms with his doppelgängers from tribute band No Way Sis. And went playfully apoplectic at the news that Noel had given his treasured guitar to No Way Sis' 'Noel' after the show. Drink was drunk. Oblivion engulfed us.

The build-up to Knebworth took tabloid interest in the band to unprecedented levels. Particularly when Noel declared that he was going to refuse the Ivor Novello Award for Best Songwriter awarded jointly to Gallagher and Damon Albarn. A foolish move perhaps, since it reignited the war of words between Oasis and Blur, but an understandable response to what always seemed like a dumb publicity gesture by the awards committee.

'Arsed,' he told me. 'I've got enough awards already. They can give me more when I move and get somewhere to put them.'

Knebworth was unreal.

The biggest British gig of all time swooped through a celebration of Being Right. And, while I'd always hated the Nuremburg manque appropriations, part and parcelled with such events, it was hard to deny the fuck-off brilliance of the event.

Creation's backstage tent had chandeliers.

Oasis were on the news ahead of at least five world leaders. It was getting out of control.

'Knebworth was something we had to do,' says Noel, 'and it was brilliant. There was a really bad bit [truck driver James Hunter getting crushed to death in front of Noel as the stage was set up] and that kind of brings you down to earth, reminds you that it's just a fucking pop concert, but, over the two nights, we played gigs that pissed on anything anyone else had ever done. The people that were there, they knew.'

Not if they were with the *Daily Mirror* they didn't. The paper's eternally bewildered pop correspondent Matthew Wright penned a grumpy diatribe about expensive burgers and long beer queues, typically, and spectacularly missing the point.

Why did Oasis play Knebworth?

Because they could.

My sister, who lives in Cambodia, is one of the few people who'd never been consumed by Oasis' cascade. She'd heard OF them, and so had the children she teaches, but never experienced the vivaciousness of their reality. In the backstage ballroom, I hung with her and Liam and Kate Moss. Out near the stage, Noel bundled me to the floor as he careered out of a helicopter.

'Who are they?' she asked.

'That's Oasis,' I let on.

Explaining the situation to Liam, he admitted that he was jealous of her.

'Imagine,' he said, 'you see Oasis for the first time and it's at Knebworth. That'd be brilliant. I wish I was her. It's like, Lennon never saw The Beatles live.'

Two hours later, I saw my sister.

'They're good,' she said.

They were.

MTV had been pestering the band for ages to do one of their

'Unplugged' showcases, a scenario that usually reiterates the futility of the no-mark losers chasing after acoustic reinventions of their own stupidity, but, just occasionally (10,000 Maniacs, Rod Stewart) reveals a cockeyed flamboyance. Oasis were supposed to just impress the Americans. That was the corporate plan.

It went weird. Surprisingly.

On 23 August, Oasis were booked into London's Royal Festival Hall to elaborate on intimacy. It wouldn't be 'unplugged' in any technical sense. It never was. It was a billboard with corporate corners.

And it didn't rock any rafters. Noel came on stage with Bonehead, Guigs and Alan.

'Sorry,' he said, 'Liam's got a sore throat. You're just going to have to put up with the ugly one.'

The bulk of the audience, battered by a yelpingly insistent American director (a woman who'd decided that everyone sitting in just the right places would be preceded by an annexation of the Sudetenland) whooped in most of the right places. Those of us who cared, did our best to pretend that Noel's interpretations of the Oasis opus could realy scrape the senses.

Liam was supposed to be ill. He didn't look that ill as he goofed about with Patsy in one of the boxes. Half way through the set, he walked on stage and me and my mates found hairs standing up on the back of our necks that we never knew existed. If ever there was a moment that it became clear that Noel was the heart of the band, but Liam was the soul, it was then.

Noel's attempt at salvage was a lot better than some have since reported. Liam's boozy denial of his responsibilities echoed the Albert Hall, 'Undrugged' gig rather too precisely, and the tabloid journalists scuttling to 'report' the occasion would have been wearily predictable if some of us hadn't squeezed chewy into all the coin slots of the venue's telephones.

It was all right. Oasis were never supposed to be all right.

On 26 August, Oasis were due to fly to America for a post-Knebworth tour, another reminder that their pan-global excursions were always going to embrace a whole continent of fans. Snidey historical revision finds press cuttings proffering cockamamey theories about how the band never toured America, never really made an effort.

This was their ninth US tour.

Half-hearted? Yeah, right.

Six months before Knebworth, it seemed like exactly the right thing for Oasis to do. If you'd have asked me as I sat watching them rehearse for the British shows (as documented in the last chapter) whether an American trip would have been advisable, I couldn't have conjured up any outlines of inadvisability. Hell, I'd have bought-in to a gig on Jupiter.

'We shouldn't have gone straight out to America,' says Liam. 'I still don't really know why we just didn't just stay in England and chill out. We'd done those gigs and after that we could have done whatever we wanted. Then, a week later, we're supposed to be going to be fucking flying thousands of miles and doing more gigs.'

The capacities of the venues Oasis were due to play in America varied between 10,000 and 40,000, but while Liam hints at a seemingly inevitably disappointment at playing to less people than Knebworth, Noel maintains the size of audience was no problem.

'I'd play to two people if they were really into us,' he says.

Maybe he would, but by September 1996, it was only ever going to seem like an excerpt of just what they could do.

Liam didn't fly out to America with them. The official excuse was that he was looking for a house. And it was a justification that held water. He really was looking for somewhere to live, aware that his life with Patsy was shaping a potential security and joy he'd never had before. He had his priorities.

He was either a self-centred, arrogant madman, or he was in

love and he was right. As someone who's only ever existed for the Everlasting Now, it's hardly surprising that he feels no remorse.

'I couldn't go out that day. End of story.'

So, for the first few American gigs, Noel reprised the 'Unplugged' scenario, fronting a couple of gigs and maintaing the charade that an Oasis without Liam was ever going to be anything more than a blurry snapshot of their capability. He did his best, and publicly defended Liam's actions ('You have to support people when they're going through a personal crisis'), but the tabloid's cartoon 'concern' never came close to the band's own realisation that things were going very, very wrong.

On September 4, Liam finally flew out to America and joined the band for the MTV Video Music Awards. He was haphazardly, if entertainingly snotty to the global factory-farmed audience, ensuring yet more column inches back home and a growing American impatience with what was seen as Brit Obscenity.

Pearl Jam and Smashing Pumpkins condemned what they saw as 'rudeness'.

Hello?


Me and Matthew, Martin and Brian from Microdot (the people who design Oasis' logo and record sleeves) flew out to New York for the two Long Island gigs. Torrential rain almost demanded their abandonment and, as we sat on stage watching Oasis distractedly going through the motions, we wished the thunderstorms had lasted that little bit longer. For the first time ever, I watched the band play and felt nothing. The audience whooped at 'Wonderwall' and slumped for the other hour and a bit.

In the dressing room afterwards, Bonehead said 'How much longer before we get out of this godforsaken country?'

Three days later in Charlotte, North Carolina, a drunken argument between Noel and Liam ('It was about Abba, I think,' offers Liam) ended with Noel flying back to Britain on Concorde and tabloids, broadsheets and TV news stations deciding that their barney was more important than people all over the world getting killed.

Liam flew back the next day, had a sandwich in a graveyard with his minders and went off to hang out with Noel in the countryside for a few days. The *Sun* engineered a deeply moronic theory about how they themselves both split up Oasis and got them back together again, clouding the reactions of those of us who actually cared.

Within days, the news filtered out. They weren't splitting up, but they weren't going to tour for the forseeable future. It was time to, like, just fucking stop, before their heads exploded.

'There was another album to do,' says Noel. 'Oasis weren't going to split up before we did that. We'd just toured too long.'

Oasis were in the papers every day, reporters laboriously outlining every trip that Noel and Liam made to the corner shop for a pint of milk or (tremendously) 200 B&H. They were the most boring thing in the world.

But there was still the album. While Noel and Alan McGee publicly endorsed Labour's pre-election campaign, it seemed like Oasis as a group might never record again.

'We were just waiting,' says Liam.

Noel kept in the limelight with his vocal contribution to the Chemical Brothers' 'Setting Sun' (a knowing nod to The Jam's 'Setting Sons' album) which made Number One in the singles chart.

On 19 October, Oasis went to Abbey Road (where else?) and started recording their third album, 'Be Here Now'. The title was taken from John Lennon's understanding of the Maharishi's teachings in Rushikesh. The sound, as the demo had already hinted, was to wrench Oasis across every face brave enough to pop above the parapet.

'It's going to be a fuck-off album,' Noel told me as they prepared to start recording. 'The same old pub-rock shit, but louder.'

The band released two boxed sets of their singles to date in giant fake Benson and Hedges boxes, design by Microsoft, pictures by Jill Furmanovsky and sleevenotes by, er, me. Keeping it in the family forever.

'We knew there wasn't going to be a single for a while,' says Johnny Hopkins from Creation. 'But you look at what they've had out so far and I'd challenge anyone to match it. With the boxed sets, you could either buy all the records in them or get the empty box with just the pamphlet and the live CD. It was a way of letting people know they were still around.'

To launch the boxed sets, Oasis, by now lazy rich fuckers or something, let their tribute band No Way Sis play the Virgin Megastore in London's Oxford Street. Meg turned up and confessed that it was weird to hear 'Wonderwall' sung to her by a crazy Scottish doppelgänger.

Oasis carried on recording at Abbey Road until tabloid attention and fan follow-ups meant that they couldn't get near the studio without getting mobbed.

After the Q Magazine awards ceremony, Liam was busted in the street with, allegedly two grammes of coke on him, and coincidentally was snapped by a *News Of The World* photographer. In the same month, the tabloids led us to believe that he was banned from the Groucho Club for smashing up a snooker table and found time to bite a girl's nose at an Ocean Colour Scene gig. Oddly enough, when the *Sun* and the *Mirror* discovered that Gallagher-baiting wasn't a smart way to win readers, the incessant muck-raking screeched to a halt. To this day, they're not quite sure whether to treat the band as threats to the nation's stability or a kind of cagouled-up replacement for the Royal Family. That the band themselves are several thousand miles away from actually giving a fuck sort of goes without saying.

At Creation Records' Christmas party at The Saint in London's West End, Liam was cheerily confident about the progress of the album.

'It was so fucking boring, not doing anything,' he confessed. 'There's all these bands around saying that we've gone away and we're finished. Fuck them. When they hear what we're doing, they might as well just give up.'

Liam was going to marry Patsy on 10 February 1997. But he didn't. The happy couple were apparently both allergic to representatives from the Big Breakfast conducting a live broadcast from outside their house. On 7 April, they married at Marylebone Registry Office. They're happy togeether and, it seems, really good for each other. Not perhaps the most blipvert friendly of arrangements, but one that has already survived the vicarious inquisitions of fat, sweaty men in kipper ties. A result of sorts.

Just after Liam got married, Smaller played London's Borderline. Their singer, Diggsy, the protagonist of Oasis' 'Diggsy's Dinner' spent hours in his room at the Columbia Hotel 'jamming' with Noel. They collaborated eventually on a great chorus that went 'I bought a bag of spanners/ from a girl who's got no manners' before the police got called and we all ran around the building like we were banned or something.

Noel was. Twice. As we hunched in a cubbyhole, he told me that Oasis were thinking of playing some gigs at the end of June in America with U2.

'Our work permits run out then,' he said, 'so we thought we'd get a couple of gigs in, then fuck off. If you keep it a secret, you can come.'

I cut my tongue off, and waited.

'Be Here Now' got finished out in the countryside, Noel magnanimously revealing that anyone could have an interview if they got 'past the bouncers and a mile down the road'. It didn't stop him coming back to London to see new bands that took his fancy like the determinedly indie Travis.

On 21 May, I saw Noel at Rolling Stone Ronnie Wood's fiftieth birthday party. Friends of mine in a band called Beautiful People (who'd been picked to play by Wood himself) had supported Oasis in '94. This time he was there to see them in the company of Damon Hill, Mick Jagger, Anita Pallenburg, Marianne Faithful and Frankie Dettori. Gallagher was the only one not in fancy dress.

Two weeks later he married Meg in Las Vegas, a ceremony that dragged in an Elvis Presley impersonator and a brace of Beatles songs. The honeymoon got delayed as Oasis clung onto that continent, articulating a cocky resurrection.

First off, a thirty minute gig at the K-ROQ radio station's, ahem, Weenie Roast, in LA, a favour to Rod 'The Mod' Biggenheimer. On the same bill as Blur (got a problem with that?) and The Chemical Brothers, they tentatively trod water, defied bootleggers by only playing old songs and pretty much coloured in a picture called Fuck All.

Three days later, they tore up clouds.

Supporting U2 at Oakland Colisseum, outside San Francisco, was never going to be the easiest of gigs, particularly since they were expected to come on stage in the late afternoon sun-shine, a soundtrack, for the first day, to 40,000 apologists for the dumbly spectacular, most of them still grumpy about Oasis' previous dismissal of corporate indifference. The crowd wanted flashy prog-rock, and they wanted it now.

'Hello, we're Oasis and we're from Manchester.'

The promoter had threatened to pull the plugs if there was any wilful antagonism, but he needn't have worried. This was Oasis rediscovering their casual brilliance, proving that even in the brutal sunshine, they could make a noise to interfere with angels.

The next night, they were better still, buoyed up by a huge Manc presence, their unashamed rock simplicity emphasising the desperate attempts by U2 to outline a glitzy future. Friendships and a certain disregard for quality control found Liam defending U2 after the event, but deep down, you could see he knew just how startlingly invigorating Oasis were.

'D'You Know What I Mean' (inspired by a Wigan phrase utilised to the point of distraction by the boys from Microdot at the 1996 Long Island gigs) and the Guns'n'Roses inspired title track from the album, 'Be Here Now' swept away any doubts about the band's capacity to still thrill.

They were good. Really good.

And now, in the San Francisco hotel bar, Liam explains what Oasis are all about.

'You fucking know, Paul. We're the best band in the world. By miles.'

Two weeks later, back in England, I have an hour long 'discussion' with him about whether it would be better to be John Lennon or George Best.

You'd rather be Oasis. 'Be Here Now' is brash, beautiful proof.

Oasis still want your soul.

# GIGOGRAPHY

All dates refer to gigs where Oasis headlined, unless otherwise noted.

**1991**
1.  18 Aug – Boardwalk, Manchester; supporting Sweet Jesus
2.  19 Oct – Boardwalk, Manchester

**1992**
3.  15 Jan – Boardwalk, Manchester
4.  19 Apr – Polytechnic, Dartford
5.  20 Apr – Hippodrome, Oldham; supporting Revenge
6.  5 May – Club 57, Oldham; supporting the Ya Ya's
7.  14 July – Boardwalk, Manchester
8.  Aug – Boardwalk, Manchester
9.  13 Sep – The Venue, Manchester; In The City 1992
10. 22 Nov – Boardwalk, Manchester; supporting the Cherries

**1993**
11. 5 Jan – Boardwalk, Manchester; supporting the Essence

12. Mar – Le Bateau, Liverpool
13. Apr – Krazy House, Liverpool
14. May – Boardwalk, Manchester
15. 31 May – King Tut's, Glasgow; supporting 18 Wheeler
16. Jun – University, Manchester; supporting Dodgy
17. Jul – Boardwalk, Manchester
18. Jul – Le Bateau, Liverpool
19. 11 Sep – Duchess, Leeds
20. 14 Sep – Canal Bar, Manchester; In The City 1993
21. 7 Oct – University, Manchester; supporting Liz Phair
22. 14 Oct – University, Manchester; supporting Milltown Brothers
23. 27 Oct – University, Keele; supporting BMX Bandits
24. 28 Oct – University, Sheffield; supporting BMX Bandits
25. 1 Nov – Warehouse, Derby; supporting BMX Bandits
26. 3 Nov – Wulfrun Hall, Wolverhampton; supporting BMX Bandits
27. 4 Nov – Powerhaus, London
28. 28 Nov – University, Sheffield; supporting CNN
29. 1 Dec – Institute, Birmingham; supporting Saint Etienne
30. 2 Dec – Plaza, Glasgow; supporting Saint Etienne
31. 4 Dec – University, Warwick
32. 8 Dec – Wulfrun Hall, Wolverhampton; supporting the Verve
33. 9 Dec – University, Manchester; supporting the Verve
34. 10 Dec – Cathouse, Glasgow; supporting the Verve
35. 11 Dec – The Mill, Preston; supporting the Verve
36. 13 Dec – Riverside, Newcastle; supporting the Verve
37. 14 Dec – King's Hall, Bradford; supporting the Verve
38. 16 Dec – Krazy House, Liverpool; supporting Real People

**1994**
39. 27 Jan – Water Rats, London
40. 6 Feb – Gleneagles, Scotland
41. 23 Mar – Angel, Bedford

42. 24 Mar – 100 Club, London
43. 26 Mar – Forum, Tunbridge Wells
44. 27 Mar – Polytechnic, Oxford
45. 28 Mar – Jug of Ale, Birmingham
46. 29 Mar – Joiners, Southampton
47. 30 Mar – Fleece and Firkin, Bristol
48. 31 Mar – Moles, Bath
49. 5 Apr – Lucifer's Mill, Dundee
50. 6 Apr – La Belle Ange, Edinburgh
51. 7 Apr – Tramway, Glasgow
52. 8 Apr – Arena, Middlesbrough
53. 11 Apr – Wheatsheaf, Stoke
54. 12 Apr – Duchess, Leeds
55. 13 Apr – Lomax, Liverpool
56. 29 Apr – Adelphi, Hull
57. 30 Apr – University, Coventry
58. 2 May – Wedgewood Rooms, Portsmouth
59. 3 May – TJ's, Newport
60. 4 May – Warehouse, Derby
61. 6 May – Charlotte, Leicester
62. 7 May – Old Trout, Windsor
63. 8 May – Roadmenders, Northampton
64. 10 May – Army & Navy, Chelmsford
65. 11 May – Boat Race, Cambridge
66. 13 May – Venue New Cross, London
67. 14 May – Leadmill, Sheffield
68. 1 Jun – Edwards 8, Birmingham
69. 2 Jun – University, Cardiff
70. 3 Jun – Island, Ilford
71. 6 Jun – Arts Centre, Norwich
72. 8 Jun – Marquee, London
73. 9 Jun – University, Manchester
74. 11 Jun – Avenham Park, Preston; festival
75. 12 Jun – Cathouse, Glasgow
76. 13 Jun – Cathouse, Glasgow

77.   16 Jun – Erotika, Paris, France
78.   18 Jun – Centre (East Wing), Brighton
79.   26 Jun – Glastonbury, Somerset; festival
80.   21 Jul – Wetlands, New York, NY
81.   31 Jul – T in the Park, Hamilton, Scotland; festival
82.   10 Aug – Irish Centre, Leeds
83.   11 Aug – Wulfrun Hall, Wolverhampton
84.   13 Aug – Hultsfred, Sweden; festival
85.   15 Aug – Rock City, Nottingham
86.   16 Aug – Forum, London
87.   18 Aug – Astoria, London
88.   28 Aug – Lowlands, Holland; festival
89.   31 Aug – Tivoli, Buckley
90.   2 Sep – Gino, Stockholm, Sweden
91.   3 Sep – Tivoli, Dublin, Ireland
92.   4 Sep – Limelight, Belfast
93.   5 Sep – Hacienda, Manchester
94.   8 Sep – Logo, Hamburg, Germany
95.   9 Sep – Arena, Amsterdam, Holland
96.   13 Sep – Quattro, Tokyo, Japan
97.   14 Sep – Quattro, Tokyo, Japan
98.   15 Sep – Quattro, Tokyo, Japan
99.   16 Sep – Quattro, Tokyo, Japan
100.  18 Sep – Quattro, Tokyo, Japan
101.  19 Sep – Quattro, Nagoya, Japan
102.  23 Sep – Moc's, Seattle, WA
103.  24 Sep – Satyricon, Portland, OR
104.  26 Sep – Bottom of the Hill, San Francisco, CA
105.  27 Sep – Melarky's, Sacramento, CA
106.  29 Sep – The Whiskey, Los Angeles, CA
107.  14 Oct – Uptown Bar, Minneapolis, MN
108.  15 Oct – Metro, Chicago, IL
109.  16 Oct – St Andrews Hall, Detroit, MI
110.  18 Oct – Grog Shop, Cleveland, OH
111.  19 Oct – Lee's Palace, Toronto, Canada

112. 21 Oct – Local 186, Allston, MA
113. 22 Oct – Met Cafe, Providence, RI
114. 23 Oct – JC Dobbs, Philadelphia, PA
115. 26 Oct – 9:30 Club, Washington, DC
116. 28 Oct – Maxwell's, Hoboken, NJ
117. 29 Oct – Wetlands, New York, NY
118. 3 Nov – Aéronef, Lille, France
119. 4 Nov – La Cigale, Paris, France
120. 5 Nov – Transbordeur, Lyons, France
121. 6 Nov – Théâtre du Moulin, Marseilles, France
122. 16 Nov – Palladium, Stockholm, Sweden
123. 17 Nov – Cue Club, Gothenburg, Sweden
124. 18 Nov – Dairy, Lund, Sweden
125. 19 Nov – Loft, Berlin, Germany
126. 21 Nov – Markthalle, Hamburg, Germany
127. 23 Nov – Batchkapp, Frankfurt, Germany
128. 24 Nov – Luxor, Cologne, Germany
129. 25 Nov – Paradiso, Amsterdam, Holland
130. 27 Nov – Zeche Carl, Essen, Germany
131. 28 Nov – Botanième, Brussels, Belgium
132. 30 Nov – Guildhall, Southampton
133. 1 Dec – Octagon, Sheffield
134. 4 Dec – Corn Exchange, Cambridge
135. 7 Dec – Barrowlands, Glasgow
136. 11 Dec – Civic Hall, Wolverhampton
137. 12 Dec – Astoria, Cardiff
138. 13 Dec – Hammersmith Palais, London
139. 17 Dec – Royal Court, Liverpool
140. 18 Dec – Academy, Manchester
141. 27 Dec – Barrowlands, Glasgow
142. 29 Dec – Centre, Brighton
143. 30 Dec – Town Hall, Middlesbrough

**1995**
144. 28 Jan – DV8, Seattle, WA

145. 29 Jan – Commodore Ballroom, Vancouver BC, Canada
146. 30 Jan – Roseland Theater, Portland, OR
147. 1 Feb – The Fillmore, San Francisco, CA
148. 3 Feb – The Palace, Hollywood, CA
149. 4 Feb – SOMA Live, San Diego, CA
150. 5 Feb – Nile Theater, Mesa, AZ
151. 7 Feb – Bar & Grill, Salt Lake City, UT
152. 9 Feb – Bluebeard Theater, Denver, CO
153. 11 Feb – Deep Ellum Live, Dallas, TX
154. 12 Feb – Liberty Lunch, Austin, TX
155. 13 Feb – Urban Art Bar, Houston, TX
156. 15 Feb – New Daisy Theater, Memphis, TN
157. 17 Feb – Cat's Cradle, Carrboro, NC
158. 18 Feb – Masquerade, Atlanta, GA
159. 3 Mar – Stone Pony, Asbury Park, NJ
160. 4 Mar – WUST Music Hall, Washington, DC
161. 5 Mar – The Abyss, Virginia Beach, VA
162. 7 Mar – Theater of the Living Arts, Philadelphia, PA
163. 8 Mar – The Academy, New York, NY
164. 10 Mar – Lupo's, Providence, RI
165. 11 Mar – Avalon, Boston, MA
166. 12 Mar – Club Soda, Montreal, Canada
167. 14 Mar – Phoenix Theater, Toronto, Canada
168. 15 Mar – The Odeon, Cleveland, OH
169. 16 Mar – St Andrews Hall, Detroit, MI
170. 18 Mar – Tyndale Armory, Indianapolis, IN
171. 19 Mar – Vic Theater, Chicago, IL
172. 20 Mar – Orbit Room, Grand Rapids, MI
173. 24 Mar – First Ave, Minneapolis, MN
174. 25 Mar – Rave at Eagles, Milwaukee, WI
175. 17 Apr – Cliffs Pavilion, Southend
176. 20 Apr – Bataclan, Paris, France
177. 22 Apr – Arena, Sheffield
178. 22 Jun – Bath Pavilion, Bath
179. 23 Jun – Glastonbury, Somerset; festival

180. 30 Jun – Roskilde Festival, Denmark
181. 3 Jul – Palalido, Milan, Italy
182. 5 Jul – Fauvier Festival, Lyons, France
183. 7 Jul – Out in the Green Festival, Frauenfeld, Switzerland
184. 8 Jul – Eurokeenes Festival, Belfort, France
185. 9 Jul – Badesee, Duren, Germany
186. 14 Jul – Beach Park, Irvine, Scotland
187. 15 Jul – Beach Park, Irvine, Scotland
188. 18 Jul – Plaza de Toros de las Ventas, Madrid, Spain
189. 21 Jul – Zeebruggers Beach Festival, Belgium
190. 22 Jul – Slane Castle, Dublin, Ireland
191. 21 Aug – Club Citta, Tokyo, Japan
192. 22 Aug – Club Citta, Tokyo, Japan
193. 23 Aug – Liquid Room, Tokyo, Japan
194. 25 Aug – Garden Hall, Tokyo, Japan
195. 26 Aug – Garden Hall, Tokyo, Japan
196. 28 Aug – Imperial Hall, Osaka, Japan
197. 29 Aug – Imperial Hall, Osaka, Japan
198. 2 Oct – Empress Ballroom, Blackpool
199. 3 Oct – Trentham Gardens, Stoke
200. 5 Oct – International Centre, Bournemouth
201. 6 Oct – Leisure Centre, Gloucester
202. 10 Oct – Hammerjack's, Baltimore, MD
203. 11 Oct – Roseland Ballroom, New York, NY
204. 13 Oct – Tuxedo Junction, Danbury, CT
205. 14 Oct – The Orpheum, Boston, MA
206. 16 Oct – Metropol, Pittsburgh, PA
207. 31 Oct – La Luna, Brussels, Belgium
208. 4 Nov – Earls Court Exhibition Centre, London
209. 5 Nov – Earls Court Exhibition Centre, London
210. 7 Nov – Zenith, Paris, France
211. 10 Nov – Grosse Freiheit, Hamburg, Germany
212. 12 Nov – Live Music Hall, Cologne, Germany
213. 14 Nov – Trocadère, Nantes, France
214. 15 Nov – Aéronef, Lille, France

215. 17 Nov – Granby Hall, Leicester
216. 20 Nov – Annexet, Stockholm, Sweden
217. 24 Nov – KB Hallen, Copenhagen, Denmark
218. 26 Nov – NYNEX Arena, Manchester
219. 2 Dec – KNDD Holiday Festival, Seattle, WA
220. 7 Dec – WHFS Holiday Festival, Washington, DC
221. 8 Dec – Q101 Holiday Festival, Chicago, IL
222. 9 Dec – KEGE Holiday Festival, Minneapolis, MN
223. 13 Dec – Liberty Warehouse, Toronto, Canada
224. 15 Dec – Live 105 Holiday Festival, San Francisco, CA
225. 16 Dec – KOME Holiday Festival, San Jose, CA
226. 18 Dec – KROQ Holiday Festival, Los Angeles, CA
227. 18 Dec – Viper Room, Hollywood, CA

**1996**
228. 10 Jan – Music Centre, Utrecht, Holland
229. 12 Jan – Munich, Germany
230. 14 Jan – Huxley's, Berlin, Germany
231. 15 Jan – Bielefeld, Germany
232. 19 Jan – Whitley Bay Ice Rink, Tyne & Wear
233. 21 Jan – Ingleston Exhibition Centre, Edinburgh
234. 22 Jan – Ingleston Exhibition Centre, Edinburgh
235. 23 Feb – Memorial Hall, Kansas City, MO
236. 24 Feb – American Theater, St Louis, MO
237. 26 Feb – Orpheum Theater, Minneapolis, MN
238. 27 Feb – Aragon Ballroom, Chicago, IL
239. 1 Mar – Eagle's Auditorium, Milwaukee, WI
240. 2 Mar – Lakewood Civic Auditorium, Cleveland, OH
241. 3 Mar – State Theater, Detroit, MI
242. 5 Mar – Egyptian Room, Indianapolis, IN
243. 7 Mar – GMU Patriot Center, Fairfax, VA
244. 9 Mar – Tower Theater, Philadelphia, PA
245. 10 Mar – Strand Theater, Providence, RI
246. 13 Mar – Paramount Theater, New York, NY
247. 18 Mar – International Arena, Cardiff

248. 19 Mar – International Arena, Cardiff
249. 22 Mar – The Point Depot, Dublin, Ireland
250. 23 Mar – The Point Depot, Dublin, Ireland
251. 26 Mar – Stadthalle, Offenbach, Germany
252. 27 Mar – Terminal 1, Munich, Germany
253. 29 Mar – Palalido, Milan, Italy
254. 31 Mar – Summum, Grenoble, France
255. 2 Apr – Zeleste, Barcelona, Spain
256. 10 Apr – Pacific Coliseum, Vancouver, Canada
257. 11 Apr – Mercer Arena, Seattle, WA
258. 13 Apr – Bill Graham Civic Auditorium, San Francisco, CA
259. 18 Apr – Mammoth, Denver, CO
260. 20 Apr – Bronco Bowl Auditorium, Dallas, TX
261. 21 Apr – Austin Music Hall, Austin, TX
262. 27 Apr – Maine Road, Manchester
263. 28 Apr – Maine Road, Manchester
264. 3 Aug – Loch Lomond, Scotland
265. 4 Aug – Loch Lomond, Scotland
266. 7 Aug – Sjohistoriska Museet, Stockholm, Sweden
267. 10 Aug – Knebworth Park, Stevenage
268. 11 Aug – Knebworth Park, Stevenage
269. 14 Aug – Pairc Ui Chaoimh, Cork, Ireland
270. 15 Aug – Pairc Ui Chaoimh, Cork, Ireland
271. 27 Aug – Horizon, Rosemont, IL
272. 28 Aug – Hara Arena, Dayton, OH
273. 31 Aug – Molson Park, Toronto, Ontario
274. 2 Sep – Corestates Center, Philadelphia, PA
275. 6 Sep – The Centrum, Worcester, MA
276. 7 Sep – Jones Beach Theatre, Long Island, NY
277. 8 Sep – Jones Beach Theatre, Long Island, NY
278. 10 Sep – Nissan Pavilion, Bristow, VA

**1997**
280. 7 Jun – Tibetan Freedom Concert, Randall's Island, NY
281. 14 Jun – KROQ Wennie Roast, Irvine, CA

282. 18 Jun – Coliseum, Oakland, CA (with U2)
283. 19 Jun – Coliseum, Oakland, CA (with U2)
284. 8 Sep – Oslo Spektrum, Norway
285. 9 Sep – Stockholm Globe, Sweden
286. 10 Sep – Copenhagen Forum, Denmark
287. 13 Sep – Westpoint Arena, Exeter
288. 14 Sep – Westpoint Arena, Exeter
289. 6 Sep – Arena, Newcastle
290. 17 Sep – Arena, Newcastle
291. 19 Sep – Exhibition and Conference Centre, Aberdeen
292. 20 Sep – Exhibition and Conference Centre, Aberdeen
293. 22 Sep – Arena, Sheffield
294. 23 Sep – Arena, Sheffield
295. 25 Sep – Earl's Court, London
296. 26 Sep – Earl's Court, London
297. 27 Sep – Earl's Court, London
298. 29 Sep – National Indoor Arena, Birmingham
299. 30 Sep – National Indoor Arena, Birmingham